YOU DON'T HAVE TO SEND YOUR CHILD TO SCHOOL

A PARENTS GUIDE TO HOME EDUCATION

by Gareth Lewis

Illustrations by
Lin & Bethan Lewis

First published 1993

Copyright (c) Gareth Lewis 1993

Primrose Lane Educational Press
P.O. Box 154
Pocklington
York YO4 1YW

A C.I.P. catalogue record for this book is available
from the British Library

ISBN 0 9522705 0 1

Printed in Great Britain by Jorvik Business Systems
South Lodge, Bolton Lane, Wilberfoss, York YO4 5NZ

CONTENTS

How can the bird that is born for joy
Sit in a cage and sing?
How can a child, when fears annoy,
But droop his tender wing,
And forget his youthful spring?

from The Schoolboy
by William Blake

ACKNOWLEDGEMENTS

Special thanks to my wife Lin for her work typing, illustrating and in the layout; to Bethan, Wendy, and Samuel for their inspiration; and to all the children whom I have met and with whom I have worked; who have demanded something better than that which is offered in school.
Between them they have coaxed me into putting pen to paper and writing this book.

INTRODUCTION

This book is not intended to be an attack upon schools themselves, but rather upon the idea that schools provide the only possible source of education for today's children.

Many children do not fit into our modern educational system and are made deeply unhappy by having to attend school throughout their formative years. Many parents believe that schools are unable to develop the intellectual and creative abilities of their children to their fullest extent, but are unaware that alternatives exist.

In fact, school is not compulsory, and parents have the right to provide a different form of education if they feel that this would be in the best interests of their children.

The first section of this book outlines the problems inherent in any school based education in an attempt to reassure parents whose children have difficulty fitting into school, that they are not abnormal.

The second section explains that every parent has a legal right to educate their own child – irrespective of their own qualifications – and the third section explains how parents can provide their children with an interesting, worthwhile and challenging education if they decide to home educate.

Over and above everything else, the author hopes that a parent reading this book will be left with the feeling that the education of their children, which may be fraught with anxiety and stress when they are at school, can be transformed into a rewarding experience of fun and discovery if they choose to work with their children at home.

Good Luck!

Gareth Lewis
October 1994

SECTION I

SCHOOLS

SCHOOLS

Children need to be educated. There are thousands, even millions, of things that they need to know before they are adequately prepared for adult life in our modern society.

The question asked by this section of the book is whether school is the best place for a child to receive this education.

Schools are a peculiar phenomenon in that they are unpopular with nearly all the children that attend them, as they were with nearly all their parents when they were young. This unpopularity has not, however, led parents to select other forms of education for their children, and schools still provide full-time education for an estimated 99·9% of the children in this country.

The origins of schools and the way in which they have come to assume such a central role in the education of our children are explored at the end of this section.

Whatever benefits schools have brought in the past, no guarantee can be given that they will provide a suitable education in the future. Parents have to weigh the advantages and disadvantages of sending their children to school in the light of present conditions.

In the United Kingdom, education is compulsory between the ages of five and sixteen. This represents eleven years of a person's life,- eleven years in which the ability to learn and acquire new skills is at a peak. If an adult were offered an eleven year training programme they would have to be convinced that it offered quite exceptional benefits before accepting. A parent owes the same duty to their child.

Before committing your child to school you should satisfy yourself that it is the best educational option available to them. The next few pages weigh the arguments for and against schools and summarise some of the principal concerns that parents have with regard to modern schools.

Some of these points apply more to one type of school than to another. Primary schools are different to Secondary schools, and schools vary according to their staff, their premises, their intake, whether they are privately or state run and the level of resources that they receive.

Certain aspects are common to all schools, however, such as children being taught in classes, grouped according to age; the following of a pre-determined curriculum; having a timetable which dictates the pattern of the week; and above all that they are an institution and require a degree of institutionalisation from the children who attend, for them to be able to operate.

Different children react very differently to conditions in school. Some appear to be quite happy to attend school, while others develop an intense dislike of school and others become disturbed if forced to attend.

All this has to be taken into account and it is up to the parents of each child to determine whether or not any particular school can provide an adequate education for each of their children.

SOCIAL ASPECTS OF SCHOOLS

Most parents give this as their prime reason
for sending their children to school. They   fear
that if their child did not go to school they would
be deprived of the chance to make friends with people
of their own age. There is, however, much more
to the social life of school than the simple chance
to make friends with one's peers, and the whole
picture must be considered before deciding whether
or not a child benefits socially from school
attendance.

PRE-SCHOOL NURSERY GROUPS
Many parents choose to send their children
to pre-school nursery. It appears that while children aged three or four years old may sometimes play
together, they are more involved in their own worlds
at that age, and do not form friendships in the
same way as older children.

The main social effect of nursery school
appears to be that the child feels abandoned by
their parents and rather confused. This effect
is lessened when the nursery has a homely atmosphere
and is run by a caring teacher upon whom the child
comes to look as a parental-type figure.

SOCIAL ASPECTS OF PRIMARY SCHOOLS
Compulsory education begins at age five.
Being separated from their family every day is a
difficult experience for any five year old child.

Many children find the atmosphere and
conditions in a primary school to be strange and
forbidding. It is quite common for children to
cry, sometimes hysterically, or to become sullen
and depressed when first left at school. This is
the first social effect of school - that of causing
a child to lose trust in the parents who have placed
them in such an inhospitable situation.

Once settled in school, children become used

to having less contact with adults than when they were at home. A teacher who is responsible for thirty children will only be spending a few minutes per day talking to each child. This sets the pattern for the main social efect of school – children become accustomed to socialising only with people of their own age. Other children, and adults, become remote and unavailable figures.

Many parents first become aware of this when their own children stop being able to play together when they begin to attend school. Brothers and sisters often develop intense rivalries and feuds which are rarely evident in home-educating families.

The rigid structuring of school means that children rapidly lose the ability to play with older and younger children. This is a great pity, because it is by playing with, and looking after, younger children that a growing child learns the skills that are later needed as a parent.

Instead, the school classroom engenders a mean-minded competitiveness, with some children constantly seeking to establish their superiority and others becoming resigned to the role of constant failure.

School children may also become alienated from the adult world – adults being associated with the type of authoritarian behaviour necessarily displayed by teachers. All adults are seen as belonging to that class of people who tell them when they may talk and when they must be quiet; when they must stand and when they must sit; when they may play and when they may not; when they may go to the toilet and when they can eat and drink. Anyone would find it onerous to be treated in such a way, and it is particularly onerous for young children who are unable to defend themselves. It is not surprising that they become withdrawn, subdued and secretive in the company of all adults.

A child's relationship with their parents also begins to deteriorate when they start to attend school. Children cannot understand why their parents do not protect them from the humiliation of life at school, and therefore have to rely on their own resources to solve any problems that they encounter.

In addition to all these difficulties, school attendance physically prevents children from mixing with the wider community during term time. They are therefore excluded from the rich diversity of life from which they could learn so much, and have to make do with the artificial social conditions of classroom and playground.

SOCIAL ASPECTS OF SECONDARY SCHOOLS

As they develop, children reach a stage where they are not so dependent upon adults for care and support. They become able to look after themselves and to make their own decisions. Adolescents need an active social life. They need to meet each other, to make friendships, to explore relationships and to come to terms with the issues of the day. This does not, however, have to be done in complete isolation from the rest of society. Indeed, input from other people, who have themselves faced the same issues only a few years previously, could be invaluable.

Unfortunately this input is rarely available. The social patterns established in primary schools are carried over to, and reinforced, in secondary schools. Pupils in different years have very little contact with each other, and alienation from the adult world becomes complete. The emphasis upon examination results within schools strengthens the competitive atmosphere and deepens the division between "successful" pupils and those that are "failures".

Secondary school pupils, therefore, have to face the complex pressures of growing up in our modern society either totally alone, or with only the support of a small group of friends, equally as bemused as themselves. It is difficult to conceive of a more harmful social situation for young people, and it is hardly surprising that so many are caught up in drugs, crime, violence, promiscuity and despair.

16

PEER GROUP PRESSURE

Young people at school feel the need to conform to the standards of their classmates. This is known as peer group pressure. When a child goes to school they are cut off from the support of their family. The teachers represent an authority that is seeking to limit the child's freedom to do what they want when they are in school. The only allies that a child has are, therefore, their classmates. If it becomes fashionable to smoke cigarettes in the class then a child faces the dilemma of either losing the support of their allies by not smoking or gaining the disapproval of their parents if they do smoke. The easiest solution is to smoke when with their classmates, but to deny it when questioned by their parents.

It may be acceptable to resist the pressure to smoke, but the same process is repeated with every new experience that impinges upon the class, from new fashions to horror videos, from drinking alcohol to petty crime. In every case they are done in secret, and to refuse to join in may make life intolerable.

Young people who do not go to school do not suffer peer group pressure. If they meet young people with whom they get on, then a friendship can develop. If the friendship leads into uncomfortable areas then they can break it. Life continues as normal.

EDUCATIONAL ASPECTS OF SCHOOLS

Parents are required by law to ensure that their children receive an education. It is accepted, almost without question, that children do receive an education at school. Whilst this may be true for some children, it is undoubtedly true that, for others, school attendance is a boring, frustrating and pointless experience of wasting time.

PRE-SCHOOL EDUCATION

This term has come to mean nursery school, but, in practice, children receive their pre-school education mainly at home. In the five years between birth and the start of compulsory education children undergo enormous changes and learn most of the basic skills of life. They learn to walk, to feed themselves and to control their bladder and bowel movements, but most importantly they learn to talk.

No other creature on earth has a spoken language remotely resembling human speech. Learning to master a language represents the greatest intellectual feat that anyone achieves in their lifetime, and yet it is achieved with ease by people who, in later life, are destined to be labelled as educational failures.

Children learn to speak at home from their parents, not because they are being taught but because of their innate desire to learn from and to mimic those with whom they live.

Not surprisingly, now that society is mainly literate, and because there is such a large quantity of printed material in people's homes, many children also learn to read before they go to school. The pre-school years are rich in educational experience in which children learn more rapidly than at any other time of their lives, without having to leave the security of their homes.

PRIMARY SCHOOL EDUCATION

Primary schools were first introduced for ordinary people about four hundred years ago. Their purpose was to teach children who came from illiterate families to read and write.

This, together with Arithmetic, has remained their main function ever since, although in recent years the National Curriculum has sought to define a role for them in laying the groundwork in other subjects as well.

Social conditions have, however, changed considerably over the past four hundred years, and it is no longer necessary for a child to attend school for them to learn to read. It is almost inconceivable that a child growing up in a home full of books, magazines, comics, letters, newspapers etc. could fail to learn to read.

In fact, school now puts obstacles in the path of children learning to read by expecting all children to attain certain standards by certain ages. Children who would normally learn at a slower rate feel humiliated by not being able to read as well as others in the class, and for them reading becomes a hated and feared activity.

This is even more true for Arithmetic. Young children love to count and enjoy the concept of numbers, but when they are put together in a classroom, and all are expected to learn addition, multiplication, fractions etc. at the same time, it is inevitable that some lose track of what is happening or are not yet ready for a certain level of work. They rapidly lose confidence and the pattern for failure in mathematics is established for life.

Young children are not suited to being taught in classes and cannot be expected to sit and absorb information given to them as one of a group. They learn better when they feel secure, are in a one-to-one situation with an adult or an older child and are involved in something that they find interesting. This sort of learning situation cannot be created by the type of institution currently known as "school".

SECONDARY SCHOOL EDUCATION

By the time that children reach secondary school they have become divided into successes and failures. Pupils are told that the main aim of their time in secondary school is to get qualifications, and yet only about twenty per cent of them will get the A levels necessary to proceed to Higher Education.

The majority of pupils leave school with qualifications that are of little use, and have every right to feel that their education has let them down.

The fact that these pupils were not suited to sitting in classrooms, listening to teachers, writing things down and looking in books does not make them any less worthwhile as human beings. You do not have to be academically successful to make a contribution to society, and to subject someone to a compulsory five years of classroom study and then to tell them that they have failed, is an affront to that person's dignity as a human being.

It must be possible to provide young people with an education that does not involve the classroom, that allows them to develop the skills and interests that they do have and that leaves them feeling that they are a success rather than a failure.

It is quite easy for the parent who chooses home education for their child, to achieve this.

Secondary schools were really designed for, and operate principally for the benefit of those children who are to get good academic qualifications. Even so, such children can become incredibly frustrated by the pace and methods of teaching that they employ. Children who are good at a subject find the pace of the classroom too slow and become bored and inattentive. They find the subject matter limited and uninspiring because it has been pared down to the essentials necessary to get as many of the class as possible through the next exam. Rather than inspiring gifted children and encouraging them to explore new areas of knowledge, school makes learning a mechanical and sterile activity. They may leave school with a few A levels but they are unlikely to have an enthusiasm and love of learning that marked the scholar, often self-taught, in former times.

There is no doubt that there is much that young people in the eleven to sixteen year old age range would benefit from learning, and whilst school allows some people to acquire some of this knowledge, it limits everyone to achieving far less than that of which they are capable.

Pupils that learn at home are able to develop their own interests at their own pace, and as a consequence can cover a larger area, at a deeper level and fulfill more of their potential than they could have done under the constraints of school.

TRAINING

It has long been accepted that not every child will leave school with good academic qualifications, and some schools, therefore, try to incorporate an element of technical training into their curricula. Unfortunately their achievements in this field are very limited and few children leave school with any really worthwhile technical training at the age of sixteen.

The problem that schools face is that they are not themselves the best places where work is done. The best place to learn about car mechanics is in a garage. The best place to learn about cooking is in a kitchen, and the best place to learn about building is on a building site. Schools cannot replicate these conditions and are therefore unable to capture the imagination of their pupils.

Pupils do not start to receive proper job training until they leave school. This is a shame. Young people between the ages of thirteen and sixteen are capable of developing a considerable level of skill in a trade or craft when given the chance. The present education system results in a great waste of time, and a lost opportunity for hundreds of thousands of young people.

DISCIPLINE AND PREPARATION FOR LIFE

Many people do not expect their children to do well at school but send them none the less so that they can acquire the discipline necessary to be able to cope with holding down a job when they grow up. There are flaws in this argument.

CORPORAL PUNISHMENT

The use of corporal punishment has gradually been reduced in schools and now it is completely banned in State schools. Teachers are not allowed to use any form of physical violence against children and other methods of punishment such as detentions are quite difficult to enforce.

As a result, modern schools are not the centres of discipline and orderliness that some parents imagine. It is commonplace for teachers to be sworn at, physically and verbally threatened and for their instructions to be ignored. Large areas of secondary education operate as an uneasy truce between pupils and staff, with neither wanting to provoke the other unnecessarily.

If pupils continued this sort of behaviour when they left school, they would not keep their jobs for more than a few days. In fact employers and the general public alike constantly criticise the attitude of school leavers, and young people have to drop the behaviour acquired at school very rapidly in order to be able to hold down a job.

PREPARATION FOR UNEMPLOYMENT?

At one time there was an enormous demand for unskilled, hardworking and dependable adults to work on assembly lines in factories, in steelworking, down the mines and in all areas of industry and commerce. This demand no longer exists. High tech machinery and computerisation have efficiently eliminated the need for unskilled labour.

In order to find and create employment in the future, people will need to have initiative and be able to adapt to new circumstances. By definition, school does not foster these qualities. It demands that pupils should comply with a pre-determined regime and not be too original or innovative in their behaviour.

In today's world this attitude of compliance is more likely to be a qualification for unemployment than for work.

PREPARATION FOR LIFE

There are, of course, more important things in life than work. In particular every parent hopes that their children will be able, one day, to make a happy marriage and to bring up happy, well-adjusted children.

The high divorce rate, the unhappiness of children caught up in parental disputes and the resulting financial and emotional hardships are very troubling aspects of modern life.

There are many pressures placed upon a family in our society which can cause it, eventually, to break up, and one of these is school. By being taken to school every day from the age of five,

a child's connection to their family is weakened.
When they grow up and have children themselves they
are more likely to view being a parent as an optional
activity that can be given up when life becomes
dificult. Being a parent is perceived as being
a .part-time occupation that can be delegated to
teachers, child-minders, care workers or one's
partner.

On the other hand, children who grow up in
a secure and loving home stand a better chance of
being able to reproduce these conditions for their
own children when they become parents.

MANNERS

Another quality that parents rate highly in
their children is that of being polite and well-
mannered. Children learn good manners, principally,
by example.

In a school it is very difficult for the staff
to be well-mannered towards the children. The
pressure of time, of having to get everyone listening
at the same time and of having "difficult" pupils
in the class, means that teachers find themselves
shouting at children and threatening them with
various forms of retribution if they do not obey.
This is the behaviour that children will copy, and
it is not surprising that they become loud-mouthed
and aggressive when at school.

FACILITIES IN SCHOOL

EDUCATIONAL FACILITIES

Schools are equipped with a range of educational facilities including laboratories, workshops, sports facilities and computers. Parents are concerned that their children would be denied the chance of using these facilities if they did not go to school.

In practice, children have quite limited access to them when they do go to school. Staff do not trust children to use any equipment unsupervised for fear of theft and vandalism, quite apart from any risk to a child's safety.

The school timetable limits time spent in Craft and Science lessons, so it is common for pupils to spend as much time taking equipment out and putting it away again, as actually using it.

The third section of this book explains how home educated children approach their work in quite a different way, taking much more responsibility upon themselves. They have access to different types of facilities and have more time to explore fully their potential.

PERSONAL FACILITIES

Schools are in an impossible dilemma with respect to the provision of toilets.

If they allow children unrestricted access to the toilets then the toilets rapidly deteriorate into an unbearable condition. Taps are left running, water is splashed everywhere, toilet paper is stolen, excrement and urine find their way onto the walls and floors, graffiti is daubed and the toilets and wash basins become vandalised. Because school is an institution, none of the children treat the toilets with the same respect that they do at home, and children that are feeling disturbed, finding themselves alone in the toilet, see the chance for revenge.

Schools, therefore, limit access to the toilets. Children may only go at certain times of day, or with express permission. Toilets are kept locked and children sometimes have to go and get toilet paper before going to the toilet.

Having to ask permission to go to the toilet can be very humiliating, especially as these conditions apply just as much in Secondary schools as they do in Primary schools.

Even with these precautions, school toilets are usually not pleasant as they represent an area of school where staff control is at its weakest.

The inability of an institution to provide adequate sanitary arrangements is a serious matter.

SCHOOL MEALS

Parents should also consider whether the conditions that prevail in a school kitchen and school canteen can match the standards of food and hygiene that they aspire to provide for their children.

Meals are usually pre-prepared and heated up on the premises. Large scale catering always involves hygiene problems, and may not be able to offer the nutrition that parents like to provide for their children.

HEALTH AND PHYSICAL FITNESS

EARLY PROBLEMS
COUGHS, COLDS AND RUNNY NOSES.
Children usually get a succession of coughs and colds when they start school. Being in a stressful situation, in close contact with other children, provides an ideal breeding ground for all manner of minor ailments.
PARASITES - WORMS AND LICE
These are now endemic in many schools, and children are often regularly reinfested with either or both.
STRESS - HEADACHES, INCONTINENCE, VOMITING, SKIN RASHES, SLEEPLESSNESS AND NIGHTMARES.
Some children become exceptionally stressed at school and suffer severe symptoms. Others display them in a milder form, usually just before term starts, when the fear of school is at its height, and in the first few weeks of term.

LATER PROBLEMS
BEHAVIOURAL DIFFICULTIES
Children who find school particularly alien to their natural inclinations sometimes develop behavioural problems. They will systematically disrupt lessons and ferment disturbances in the playground. They are usually referred to Educational Psychologists, and may be sent to a special school if they cannot be managed in a "normal" school.
DEPRESSION AND SUICIDE
Serious depression is now very common among young people, and the number of teenage suicides is increasing.

PHYSICAL FITNESS
Keeping children sitting behind desks for much of the day is bad for their general state of fitness, as well as leading to problems with posture. Schools have attempted to remedy this by introducing movement into the school day in the form of gym and games.

27

QUALIFICATIONS

Many parents are concerned that their children should get good qualifications, and they see school as the easiest way of achieving this. The main qualifications gained at school are GCSE's and 'A' levels.

GCSEs

These are taken at the completion of compulsory education by sixteen year olds. When jobs are scarce many pupils stay on for an extra year to resit GCSEs in an attempt to get better grades.

GCSEs were introduced to replace 'O' levels and CSEs because it was felt that pupils with CSE passes were not taken seriously by employers. An A,B or C grade in GCSE is, in theory, equivalent to an old 'O' level pass. GCSEs, unlike 'O' levels, often involve practical work and continual assessment in an effort to get away from the problems associated with examination based qualifications.

The government, employers, universities and other interested parties find it difficult to agree on the merits of the new system. Universities prefer exam based assessment, but employers prefer candidates who have some practical skills.

"A" LEVEL s

These are the key to Higher Education at University and to management and professional jobs.

They do not fall within the compass of compulsory education because pupils usually study for them between the ages of sixteen and eighteen.

'A' level courses are offered by school sixth forms, Sixth Form Colleges, Colleges of Further Education (Technical colleges), Adult Education Centres (evening classes) and correspondence courses.

PROBLEMS INHERENT IN EXAMINATIONS AT AGE SIXTEEN.

A problem with GCSEs is that they automatically brand over sixty per cent of children as being failures. When the number of sixteen year olds who pass five or more GCSE at A,B or C level starts to aproach 40% then it is assumed that standards have fallen and the grades are not really deserved. GCSEs, like 'O' levels before them, are primarily a selection process. They do not qualify a pupil for a particular job but they select those who are eligible to go on to study for 'A' level.

OVERAMBITIOUS PARENTS

Many parents feel that their children must pass this selection procedure in order to make their way in life. Some independent schools and some state schools in affluent suburban areas manage to get almost one hundred per cent of their pupils to pass five or more GCSEs with grades A,B or C.

Amongst these children there must be many who have no interest in this type of work and have only achieved these results as a consequence of constant pressure from home and school.

For such a child, school work can become a nightmare, and fear of failure becomes associated with a fear of losing the love of their parents. The child loses all sight of the subjects that interest them, and it may be not until they reach middle age, if ever, that they start to work on things that they are really good at and which they enjoy.

QUALIFICATIONS INCREASE EARNING POWER...............

Children who do possess five GCSEs with high grades can go on to study for 'A' levels, and if they pass can go on to higher education.

Qualifications from higher education open the door to training in the professions. These include:- Medicine, Dentistry, Accountancy, Architecture, Teaching etc.

At one time most of these professions had respectable training programmes open to sixteen year old school leavers who could work their way up within the profession, but now a University degree is either required or looked upon as being superior.

When practised for a long time, these types of work offer high rates of pay and, in the past, almost guaranteed employment. Parents are therefore very keen for their children to get higher qualifications and to gain entry into one of these professions.

One point that should be borne in mind is that whilst doctors, solicitors, teachers etc. do a very useful job, they are not themselves involved in the process of creating wealth. They do not grow anything or make anything.

If everyone joined these professions then there would be nothing to eat, nothing to buy and no money.

It is therefore illogical for everyone to want their children to enter these professions, and the education system is unbalanced in making these professions the pinnacle towards which everyone strives.

.... BUT NOT FREEDOM OF CHOICE.

Parents tell their children that working for their exams will increase their options in the future. This is not true.

Education, in the broadest sense, and a wealth of varied experience, do increase a person's ability to adapt to new circumstances and take on a variety of challenges; qualifications do not.

In order to pass a succession of more specialised exams a student has to become more narrow in his or her outlook, and more stereotyped in his or her views.

The professions, previously discussed, require applicants to undergo a training course that lasts for many years and, even then, offer relatively low rates of pay to those on the first rungs of the career ladder.

In order to achieve the really large salaries earned by some doctors, accountants and solicitors, a person will need an unbroken career spanning maybe thirty years.

People that break their career to have children, to travel or to try other sorts of work, may find it dificult to reenter the profession and will definitely find it very difficult to reach the top levels.

Someone who has passed their 'A' levels, gone to University and gained a degree, studied for and passed professional examinations and worked in a profession for a few years would find it very difficult to find work other than in that profession. In order to remain in the profession they may find that they have to move away from friends and relatives to a different part of the country or even abroad.

Qualifications, in the past, have offered people a chance of financial security but never greater freedom. Professional people are only assured of a good income if society in general is prosperous. When it is not, they may be less able to cope than people with wider experience and more independence of spirit.

BULLYING AND BAD LANGUAGE

Bullying is a problem created by schools and which appears to be getting worse.

BULLYING BY OLDER CHILDREN

It can be very frightening for a child to be threatened by someone older than themselves, because they are unable to judge how likely that person is to carry out the threat, and they cannot protect themselves from physical attack. However, this type of bullying can usually be stopped if the child appeals to the authority of either parent or teacher.

BULLYING BY CHILDREN IN THE SAME CLASS

This can cause much more serious problems. A bully can turn the whole class against their victim who is then subjected to a remorseless barrage of verbal, mental and sometimes physical abuse. Their life in school becomes unbearable, but they are frightened to complain to an adult for fear of alienating their classmates. This situation often results in severe "psychosomatic" illnesses causing the child to miss long periods of school, thereby weakening further their position in the class and making them an easier target for abuse.

Even when this type of bullying is exposed, the school is often unable to stop it happening. It is usually impractical to move the bully or bullies to a different class and, while they remain, the misery of their victim continues. The child who has been bullied feels that they are to blame and it is they who are responsible for causing difficulties for the staff. A sense of guilt is added to their misery.

BULLYING BY TEACHERS

Sometimes a member of staff oversteps the boundary of acceptable behaviour towards a particular

child in such a way that it can only be described
as bullying.

BAD LANGUAGE

Few parents bring their children up to swear,
and yet bad language is the rule rather than the
exception amongst school children.

The process usually starts in the earliest
years of school with children talking about bottoms
and toilets, but the language rapidly becomes cruder,
and by the time that they reach secondary school
they will be familiar with the most vulgar language
that it is possible to imagine.

Children are quite used to employing one type
of language while at school with their peers. and
a much more respectable form of speaking when at
home or with adults.

This graphically demonstrates the way in which
children have become divorced from the rest of
society. Schoolchildren develop the use of bad
language to prove that their spirit has not been
broken and that they are still capable of rebellion.
Because they are unable to assert their independence
by choosing what to do and when to do it, they have
to show their independence by being rude and using
swear words.

It is upsetting to hear children using bad
language and it is also harmful to **them**. Swearing
derives most of its inspiration from sexual per-
versions and the demeaning of sex. Using swear
words to talk about sex makes it impossible to link
it to ideas of love and affection; instead it can
only be conceived of in terms of lust and abuse.

It is disturbing to think that children are
growing up with a vocabulary of swear words that
they use to talk about sex amongst themselves, and
which forms their basis of knowledge as they reach
sexual maturity.

In the same way, swear words lend themselves
to racist and bigoted viewpoints and sound most
impressive when being used to abuse and humiliate
others.

The sort of language prevalent in schools
is a particularly ugly and worrying aspect of the
effect that schools have on children.

ADOLESCENCE

It has become accepted in our society that teenagers are difficult to cope with and that there is a serious risk of their becoming involved in some of the darker aspects of life.

They are characterised as being rude, sullen, uncooperative and secretive about their activities. Some of the most serious problems of society, such as drug abuse and crime, are more prevalent amongst teenagers than in any other age group.

It is not inevitable that the teenage years should be afflicted by such turmoil. Whilst children are powerless in the hands of adults and have to endure whatever injustices are heaped upon them, adolescents are young adults and can assert their own rights. Most children feel school to be an injustice forced upon them. When they become adolescents they make a stand against the parents and teachers who have forced them to attend (even if they decide to see it through in order to get "qualifications").

Being an adolescent in our society is not easy under any circumstances. Coming to terms with sexuality, forming opinions on religion, politics and morals, and deciding upon a career, are difficult enough when you have the support of people who have been through the same process themselves.

When you decide to reject the help of parents and other adults because your years at school have made you feel distant from them, then you have only your friends to turn to and they are often as ignorant as you.

34

CIGARETTES, ALCOHOL, CANNABIS, AMPHETAMINES, HEROIN AND OTHER DRUGS

To a growing child, all these substances fall into the same category – they are reputed to be fun but children are not meant to take them.

As the child enters adolescence, the idea that the substances are fun assumes more prominence, and the thought that they are not available causes anger and resentment.

Some young people are convinced by the idea that smoking is bad for the health but do enjoy experimenting with alcohol. Others are attracted by the association that cannabis and LSD have with the rebellious Sixties, while others may find that amphetamines help them to keep going all night at parties.

They may feel that they have to take drugs in order to keep in with their friends. Drug taking is done secretly, without the knowledge of adults, and experiments will inevitably lead to occasionally taking a total excess – which may even be life-threatening.

CRIME

It is very disturbing to live in a society that displays great wealth, in which there are shops crammed with goods of every type and description, and yet to have no money with which to buy anything.

This is the situation in which most young people find themselves. They are not paid for their enforced attendance at school, and part-time work is poorly paid and prevents them spending their free time as they would wish.

The solution for some young people is shop-lifting, breaking into people's houses and "car crimes". This is, of course, deplorable, and undermines the very foundations of civilised life, but teenagers will continue to turn to crime whilst they feel themselves to be in such a hopeless situation.

"ADULT VIDEOS"

Teenagers have access to "adult videos" and other similar material at each other's houses. Scenes of appalling and sickening violence are depicted which can cause them to lose sleep and have nightmares. They are reluctant to discuss such problems for fear of appearing weak in front of their friends, and for fear of giving away how they came to see the material, which may only be available on the black market.

TRUANCY

Truancy becomes more common in the later years of secondary education and is common in some schools.

Children who truant on their own usually try to keep a low profile, and do not usually cause trouble. It is worrying, however, to think of them hanging around the streets or sitting in cafes waiting for the end of afternoon school.

Children who truant in groups often encourage each other to perform foolish acts of daring and bravado. It is common for them to become involved in petty crime and alcohol and drug abuse.

SEX

Sex should not normally be classed as a **problem** of adolescence but, unfortunately, to many young people, it is.

The most important aspect of education in the widest sense is the teaching of a growing child about the nature of reproduction and the successful rearing of children, so that one day if they themselves have children they will bring them up in a caring and responsible manner.

In order for a child to receive this education he or she has to learn about sex in the context of its being part of a loving and caring relationship. They have to learn that sex is not simply a matter of personal gratification or a means of exerting power over someone else, and they must themselves feel free from sexual pressure. Both boys and girls can become neurotic if they feel that they are backward in this area.

36

In addition, young people today have to have a clear and precise technical understanding of such questions as protection and contraception, Venereal disease and AIDS.

It is in the area of sex education that pupils take least notice of their teachers, are most unable to talk to their parents and rely totally on each. other for knowledge.

This can, and does, have disastrous consequences. Many girls are confused about the distinction between contraceptive methods that protect against AIDS, and those which just prevent pregnancy. Many boys and girls are too embarrassed to buy, or ask for, contraceptives, but not too shy to have sex. Young people often don't make a connection between sex and pregnancy until it is too late.

An obsession with pornographic material often leads boys to treat girlfriends in an exploitative or maybe even brutal manner.

Many young people are tortured, day and night, by a sense of failure and hopelessness because they have not had any sexual experiences - even when they are only fifteen or sixteen years old.

Not all teenagers become heavily involved in drinking, drugs, sex and crime, but these issues do touch all their lives, and they do have to decide how to deal with them. The way in which they deal with them is largely determined by their upbringing and their previous experiences. School has a detrimental influence in that it helps to isolate children from the rest of the community, and forces them to be over-dependent upon each other for support.

SCHOOL PHOBIA

This is a problem with which only a few parents have to deal. It is a term that is used to describe children in whom the normal dislike of school has developed into an inability to tolerate anything to do with school.

Some children are physically sick whenever they enter a school building, will injure themselves in their attempts to escape and if restrained, will collapse into uncontrollable weeping or hysterics, and may even pass out.

"School phobic" children will run away from school at the earliest opportunity and have to be constantly watched, in order to keep them in school.

Different Local Authorities will deal with this situation differently, but there is a general asumption that there is something wrong with a school phobic child, and that given proper help and treatment, the time will come when they will be able to attend school again.

Although such children are certainly displaying an extreme reaction, there is no fundamental reason why all children **should** be able to go to school. An inability to be able to withstand school does not mean that a child will not be able to find a fulfilling role in life when an adult.

There are many situations in life and forms of employment that bear no relationship to the conditions in school, and in which a "school phobic" child may prosper, when they grow up.

Parents who are experiencing extreme difficulty in persuading their children to attend school should consider the possibility that school is the wrong educational environment for their child, and make other arrangements.

STATE SCHOOLS AND INDEPENDENT SCHOOLS

Britain is unusual in that it has a highly fragmented system of education. This is due to the historical development of the education system, with the churches, the aristocracy, industrialists and local authorities all running separate types of school. This has led to there now being a broad choice between fee-paying Independent schools and state-funded schools.

INDEPENDENT SCHOOLS

Apart from the special problems associated with boarding schools, these schools are largely free from the lawlessness and anarchy that pervades some of the schools in the state sector.

They are generally better funded and have more staff. Their reputations are based on examination results, and pupils generally experience considerable pressure to achieve academic success.

They are elitist in that they are usually only open to children whose parents can afford the fees, and pupils therefore usually leave with a rather unbalanced view of life.

STATE-FUNDED SCHOOLS

Most of these are funded by local authorities, but in an effort to recapture the old grammar school ethos, the government is encouraging them to become Grant Maintained — where they control their own spending and can select pupils.

Comprehensive schools are attended by pupils from a wide section of society, resulting in pupils gaining a better perspective of life. Lack of funds, combined with all the problems associated with school that have already been discussed, can make them very difficult places in which to be.

Many parents feel that Independent schools are better, but often unaffordable. This book argues that all schools have fundamental weaknesses, and that, for many children, the best option is to be educated out of school altogether.

ECONOMICS AND CONVENIENCE

For many parents, the idea of not having their children at school represents a complete loss of their own personal freedom. They look forward to the time when their children are old enough to go to school, and they dread the holidays.

Many parents feel that both parents have to work in order for them to survive, and single parents often cannot cope with the idea of their children being at home all the time.

This is a pity because children are not young for very long, they grow up and leave home before you know it, and the care and affection that you give them in the early years of their life stays with them always.

INCOME

Most mothers use the time that their children are at school to find a job and earn some money.

Unfortunately, most jobs do not fit in with the hours of school or holidays, and employers are not sympathetic to time being taken off when children are ill. Mothers therefore have either to take very poorly paid part-time work, or else be prepared to leave their children in the care of other people for much longer than just the school hours.

Some people believe that the extra money brought into the family in this way improves the standard of life for their children. Although children do like to have new toys, sweets, bicycles, computers and holidays, they value time spent with their parents much more highly, especially when that time is spent in talking, walking and learning together.

Much of the pressure that children experience to acquire material things comes from the playground and the need to keep up with the other children. Children who don't go to school are unaware of such pressure.

CONVENIENCE

In addition to economic considerations, many parents think that it is more convenient to send their children to school, and that having them at home all the time would be unbearably stressful.

In fact, the convenience aspect of school is largely illusory. Having to enforce regular school attendance introduces considerable stress and discord into many families and, during term time, the routine of family life is dictated by the need to get children to and from school at particular times.

Parents who do not send their children to school not only benefit from a more relaxed and harmonious relationship with their children, but also experience considerably more freedom in being able to organise their lives in a way suitable to themselves.

WEIGHING UP THE ARGUMENTS

Having considered the issues discussed over the previous pages, and having taken into account your own experience of school and the experiences of your children, you may wish to draw up a table summarising the advantages and disadvantages for your own children.

The arguments, as they have been outlined, are summarised in one such table overleaf. It is written from the perspective of the parent, as it is the parents' responsibility to choose the most appropriate education for their child. It may, however, be instructive to try and rewrite the table from your child's point of view!

Advantages of School	Disadvantages of School
My child will meet other children	My child will be subjected to peer group pressure and may be bullied. They may become alienated from other sections of society.
My child may get good qualifications.	My child will not receive much personal attention and may seriously under-achieve. They may be put off edu-cation for life.
My child may be prepared for life in the outside world.	My child will be institutionalised and have their individuality suppressed. They will be introduced to - bad language - drugs - smoking - pornography - alcohol - horror videos
My child may learn a skill useful for work.	My child may be made ill by stress; may learn bad habits in relation to work and may leave after 11 years with no useful qual-ifications.

THE ORIGINS OF SCHOOL

The table opposite starkly sums up the truth about schools. They do provide an education for children. But it is not an education that allows a child to ask questions, to be original, to develop unusual gifts, to freely express themselves or to challenge established ideas. From a social viewpoint schools have all the disadvantages inherent in an institution, and are unable to cultivate such virtues as caring for others, working together in a cooperative spirit and accepting personal responsibility for one's actions.

This being the case it is remarkable that schools have such a stranglehold on educational thinking in this country. In order to see how this situation has arisen, it is interesting to look at the history of schools in Britain.

By no means have schools been the main means of education for much of recorded history. It has always been more common for boys and girls to acquire the skills that they will need in later life, through practical experience, working with people skilled in these tasks, often within the family.

The first British schools were believed to have been established by the Romans during the first century A.D.

Prior to that there was a considerable degree of culture and civilisation in Britain, as evidenced by monuments such as Stonehenge and Avebury, the huge tin mines in Cornwall and the remains of extensive agriculture over much of the country.

There was, however, no written language, and it appears that learning was passed on by word of mouth, and not by formal schooling.

The following pages describe the schools brought to Britain by the Romans, and how these have gradually evolved into the type of institution with which we are familiar today.

SCHOOLS IN ROMAN BRITAIN

The system of schools that the Romans established throughout their empire was mainly copied from the Greeks, and can be summarised as follows

LUDUS - Elementary School.

Here, boys from the age of about six learnt to read, to write and to do simple arithmetic on their fingers or on an abacus.

These schools were for the sons of Roman citizens, and differed from our Primary schools in that all the pupils were in one room and many of them had an attendant (a pedagogue) with them, who helped them with their work i.e. as well as there being a "School master", each boy had a private tutor as well!

GRAMMATICUS - Grammar School

Some boys would go on to the Grammar School at the age of twelve or thirteen. They would read the works of great authors in Greek and Latin, concentrating upon acquiring a mastery of Grammar.

HIGHER EDUCATION

Those young men who wished to hold public office then went on to higher education where they learnt the art of speaking in public.

They studied rhetoric, grammar, dialectic, arithmetic, geometry, music and astronomy. This curriculum was later to be copied by the Roman Catholic church and to remain almost unaltered until the Reformation in the sixteenth century.

TRAINING AND QUALIFICATIONS

The basic skills taught in the Elementary school were of general use to the better -off Roman citizens - although the majority of people living in Roman Britain had no call to read or write, or even to speak Latin.

The Grammar school provided the skill in Latin required to fill administrative posts within the Empire, and the higher education equipped a young man to take up a more illustrious position if his family connections were sufficient to secure him a good start in life.

The school system existed to teach boys Latin and hence to ensure that Britain could be efficiently run as part of the Roman Empire.

GIRLS

Girls did not go to school and they did not hold official positions in the administration when they grew up. If they learnt to read and write then they did so at home. Their education was centred around learning to run a home efficiently, and obviously varied according to the social standing of their family. They learnt at home. It is only a modern perspective that makes this form of education seem inferior to that received by the boys.

CRAFTSMEN, BUILDERS, ENGINEERS, SOLDIERS AND FARMERS.

Most of the skills which we now associate with ancient Rome such as road building, construction and military tactics were not taught at school. They were learnt through practical experience Boys, working as apprentices for master craftsmen, or as soldiers in the legions, acquired these skills over the course of their working lives.

45

SCHOOLS IN MEDIEVAL BRITAIN

THE AGE OF CHIVALRY

When the Romans finally left Britain in 410 A.D. all the schools were closed. For the next few hundred years young men of noble blood were taught by their mothers to read and write. After the age of seven they joined the household of the nearest Lord as a page, and were instructed in the culture of the times by the women of the house. When they were fourteen they became knights and joined the men in their activities.

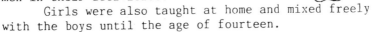

Girls were also taught at home and mixed freely with the boys until the age of fourteen.

This period of history has become known as ''the age of chivalry'' when, in theory at least, knights were taught to treat women with courtesy and respect. Maybe it is no coincidence that it corresponds to a time when education took place in the home, and was the responsibility of wives and mothers!

CHURCH SCHOOLS

In 597 A.D. St Augustine was sent by the Pope to reintroduce the Roman Catholic church to the British Isles which had had no direct contact with Rome for nearly two hundred years.

He realised that the Roman church could not become established without a supply of priests who were fluent in Latin.

The year after his arrival, St Augustine established a Grammar School in Canterbury. The curriculum was identical to that which had existed in Roman schools, and its purpose was to produce Latin scholars suitable for the priesthood.

Similar schools were attached to each cathedral as they became established.

THE COMMON PEOPLE

The Church Schools were only open to the sons of the nobility, not to girls and not to the common people.  The skills for the successful management of a rural economy continued to be passed from father to son and from mother to daughter in the time-honoured fashion.

PUBLIC SCHOOLS

This system of education continued with hardly any variation for almost a thousand years. King Alfred introduced the practice of translating Latin into English, but this largely died out with the Viking invasions.

After 1066, English disappeared completely from school work and was replaced by the practice of learning to translate Latin into French.

The first Public Schools, Winchester and Eton, were established around 1400. These were the same as the Grammar Schools except that they were not directly controlled by the Church and were independently endowed with land and buildings by their founders.

THE RENAISSANCE AND REFORMATION

THE RENAISSANCE

Remarkable changes swept across Europe during the fifteenth and sixteenth centuries.

There was a widespread rejection of the stale and implausable doctrine that the Church had been preaching without alteration for hundreds of years.

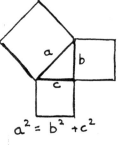

$$a^2 = b^2 + c^2$$

Scholars started to search for original Greek and Roman texts in an effort to rediscover a lost and ancient wisdom.

Under this impetus the study of mathematics, astronomy, medicine and art was revitalised and many religious doctrines were questioned.

Much of this activity, however, happened in the emerging Universities. The only change that took place in the schools was that a study of Greek was added to the study of Latin, - making them more like the old Roman schools rather than less.

They remained open only to sons of wealthy citizens, and were still principally for the training of priests for whom, by this time, there was great demand.

THE REFORMATION

When Henry Vlll broke the ties of England and Wales to Rome in the 1530's, and John Knox led Scotland to leave the Catholic Church in 1560, the power of the established Church in the British Isles was severely shaken.

This had an immediate effect upon education. The Church was forced to accept more lay people into its Grammar schools as it now needed the income brought in by school fees. This gave rise to an educated class, not directly working for the Church, who developed an interest in philosophy and science.

PRIMARY SCHOOLS (1600 onwards)

More importantly, perhaps, the Reformation brought the beginning of school for ordinary people.

The break with the Roman Church led to the use of English in church services and an English translation of the Bible.

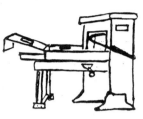

The advent of the printing press resulted in a greater availability of books - particularly the Bible.

A combination of these factors gave rise to a movement calling for ordinary people to be able to read.

Every parish was urged to establish a Primary School so that all children could learn to read, and the idea seemed to catch particular hold amongst the Nonconformist churches, especially the Quakers. These schools were open to both boys and girls but a small fee was required in order for a child to attend. Many parents did not see a need for their children to learn to read, and consequently did not send them to school.

THE INDUSTRIAL REVOLUTION

The Industrial Revolution is considered to have begun in the 1760's. Changes had been taking place gradually in the education system since about 1600, but the advent of factories and new working practices caused these changes to be dramatically accelerated.

PRIMARY SCHOOLS
The schools which taught the children of poor people to read and write took on a new importance. Previously, their motivation had been charitable and idealistic – aiming to improve the minds of ordinary people so that they could study the Scriptures for themselves. Now, however, they were seen as an important factor in the economic development of the country for the following reasons

– the better educated members of the Nonconformist churches adapted more readily to new working conditions, and were more successful in the early stages of the Industrial Revolution.

– mill owners found that children who were accustomed to running freely on the moors and in the fields did not adapt to factory conditions. A strict school regime, on the other hand, broke them in for work.

– as families moved to towns and cities to work in factories it became impossible to care for children in the traditional way. The activities available to a child in a rural community did not exist in the developing cities. Children had to be sent to school to keep them out of trouble.

SECONDARY EDUCATION

No formal schooling existed for ordinary people once they had left Primary School at the age of about twelve.

The developments in Engineering and Mechanics that led to the Industrial Revolution were usually made by craftsmen who had learnt their skills through apprenticeship and practical experience.

However, as a large working-class population grew up in the cities, people started to demand more education. The popular movements of the eighteenth and nineteenth centuries, such as the Chartists the Trade Unionists, the Mechanics Institutes and the Cooperative movement, all encouraged and supported adult education programmes. These programmes taught Science, Mathematics, Mechanics and any other subjects that people were keen to learn.

PUBLIC SCHOOLS

Throughout all this social turmoil the Public Schools and the Grammar Schools continued with hardly any changes. They continued to teach Latin and Greek, and more or less retained the curriculum of the old Roman schools.

In addition to training people for the priesthood, they educated boys from the upper classes who then went on the careers in the Civil Service, the Army and the various organs of the British Empire.

There was no way of graduating from a Primary School into one of these schools. The rigid class structure of the time was reflected in the education system.

COMPULSORY PRIMARY EDUCATION

Primary education became compulsory throughout England and Wales in 1902. Prior to that, the Education Act of 1870 had required Local Authorities to provide Primary Schools in areas where there were none.

Primary Schools were provided by a wide range of different bodies. The Churches and religious charities traditionally ran Primary Schools, particularly in country areas. In cities some industrialists provided "free" schools for their workers' children, and there were a host of dame schools, usually run by single women, that provided cheap schooling. Standards varied enormously and there was very little overall regulation of the system.

Gradually, however, the Government was persuaded to put money into schools, and in order for a school to qualify for funding its pupils had to pass an examination by an Inspector. In this way the existing schools were gradually brought together to form the system that we have today.

The 1902 Education Act established the Local Education Authorities and made them responsible for the funding and monitoring of schools.

SECONDARY SCHOOLS

Local Education Authorities were also required to offer Secondary Education to children who did well in Primary School. They did this by taking over Church-run Grammar Schools, establishing new Grammar Schools and providing scholarships to Independent Schools.

Children who did not do particularly well at Primary School, or whose parents did not want them to go to Grammar School, left school and started work when they were about twelve.

The new Grammar Schools started to abandon the traditional curriculum, and introduced modern subjects such as Science, History, Geography and Modern Languages.

THE 1944 EDUCATION ACT

This notorious Act of Parliament was conceived in a spirit of idealism, but in practice has resulted in misery for many thousands of people.

The Act was founded on the belief that schooling was beneficial, and that therefore everyone should be given compulsory education up to the age of fifteen (which was later extended to sixteen).

It was assumed that some pupils would not attain a Grammar School level of academic achievement and a new type of school was therefore invented. This was called the Secondary Modern School.

It was intended that the Secondary Modern School should concentrate upon technical and manual training, while Grammar Schools continued to provide academic training. Unfortunately, Secondary Modern Schools failed to live up to expectations. An overwhelming proportion of their pupils were left with a sense of failure and underachievement.

This has since been attributed to lack of planning, underfunding and the inability of those in authority to understand the needs of ordinary people.

It is possible, however, that School has nothing to offer a non-academic person beyond teaching them to read, write and do simple arithmetic, which they can easily learn before the age of eleven. Other skills are best learnt in the real world.

COMPREHENSIVE SCHOOLS

The two tier system of Grammar Schools and Secondary Modern Schools was so manifestly unfair that it soon lost favour politically. As a result, Comprehensive Schools were introduced during the Sixties and Seventies.

Inevitably the academic pupils who would have done well in a Grammar School found that their chances of success were considerably reduced when they had to go to school with pupils whose families

53

had no history of Secondary Education, and who themselves saw no benefit in it. Most pupils in Comprehensive Schools do not go on to study for 'A'
levels or go to University, and most Comprehensives
find it difficult to maintain an atmosphere that
encourages pupils to put school work before everything else.

Ambitious parents, therefore, found ways of
sending their children to the remaining Grammar
Schools, paying for education in an Independent
School or else making sure that their children went
to a Comprehensive School situated in an affluent
middle-class area, which was almost equivalent to
a Grammar School.

In practice, therefore, Comprehensives have
been unable to alter radically the two tier system
of education that enables children from wealthy,
ambitious families to get good qualifications, whilst
others have to put up with schools of dubious
quality.

RECENT DEVELOPMENTS

The deficiencies in the Comprehensive system
of education has led the Government to try to
institute more changes and refinements.

City Technology Colleges have been provided
with high levels of funding in an attempt to establish successful State Schools in inner city areas.

Other schools are encouraged to opt out of
Local Authority control and to become Grant Maintained. This allows them to develop their own
selection procedure for pupils, if they wish.

In another innovation, statistics are being
released showing examination results from different
schools. This encourages ambitious parents to choose
certain schools which can then select the most "able"
pupils so that they can maintain high levels of
examination passes.

Most of this activity would appear to have
the effect of making certain schools more elitist
and therefore doing nothing for the majority of
young people.

54

The trend in Secondary education since the last war has been to put more and more emphasis on the importance of examination results.

Examination results have limited significance for many young people, and do not necessarily help in either finding a job or in being competent to succeed in it.

Many young people require a broader education than can be offered by an institution that has a blinkered obsession with examinations.

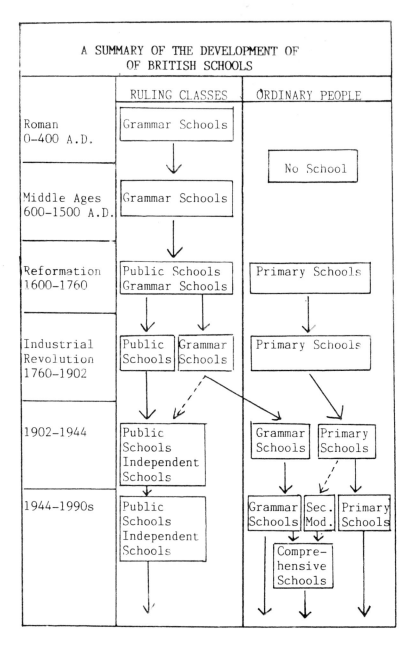

A SUMMARY OF THE DEVELOPMENT OF
OF BRITISH SCHOOLS

	RULING CLASSES	ORDINARY PEOPLE
Roman 0-400 A.D.	Grammar Schools	
		No School
Middle Ages 600-1500 A.D.	Grammar Schools	
Reformation 1600-1760	Public Schools Grammar Schools	Primary Schools
Industrial Revolution 1760-1902	Public Schools / Grammar Schools	Primary Schools
1902-1944	Public Schools Independent Schools	Grammar Schools / Primary Schools
1944-1990s	Public Schools Independent Schools	Grammar Schools / Sec. Mod. / Primary Schools / Comprehensive Schools

56

SCHOOLS - A SUMMARY

PRIMARY SCHOOLS

These were initially developed to bring about a change in the life of ordinary people i.e. to teach them to read and write.

Now that this has been achieved and we live in a society in which almost everyone can read, schools are no longer needed to fulfil this function. Children can now learn to read and write without going to school.

During the Industrial Revolution, Primary Schools also served the purpose of breaking the spirit of young children so that they would be prepared to submit to monotonous and unhealthy work when they grew up. Such working conditions no longer exist to any great extent and, faced with an uncertain future, children need an education that allows them to retain their individuality, their creativity and their enthusiasm. Primary Schools are clearly inappropriate for this.

SECONDARY SCHOOLS

These have existed since Roman times and their traditional function was to educate a privileged elite (nearly always male) to take up key posts in the administration of the country.

This is an uncomfortable role for State-run schools, especially in a society that is trying to move away from a rigid class structure.

Some children do gain qualifications from school which enable them to go on to well-paid professional jobs. These qualifications can be gained with less trauma to child and parent outside of the school system if a child is allowed to develop their own interests, and then to work seriously for examinations when they become clear as to which career they wish to follow.

The majority of children do not gain useful qualifications from Secondary School and are in

compulsory, full-time education because society
is unable to offer them useful work.

Most young people in this position see their
live years in Secondary School as a complete waste
of time.

INDEPENDENT SCHOOLS

These have retained their place in British
life because they are able to achieve high examination results. This is done with the aid of more
resources than are available to State Schools, and
by relentless pressure being applied to the child.

This type of education may have helped children
to be able to enter the Professions in the past,
but there is no guarantee that such a single-minded
commitment to examination passes is the key to
success in the future.

SECTION II

FIRST STEPS IN
HOME EDUCATION

THE ALTERNATIVES TO SCHOOL

WHAT IS SCHOOL?

The legal definition of a school is that it is an institution which provides full-time education for five or more children of compulsory school age. It is possible, however, to imagine a place which falls within this definition but which does not have all the drawbacks discussed in the previous section.

In order to look at all the alternatives to school, it is useful to be able to identify the aspects of schools that cause them to be so intolerable to so many children.

These may be summarised as follows

COMPULSION

Many children do not want to go to school and are forced to attend against their will. Young children often simply prefer the security and loving atmosphere at home, whilst older children can come to see the work that they have to do at school as being pointless. However valid a reason a child has for not wanting to go to school, they are nearly always compelled to attend.

This compulsion poisons the atmosphere in schools and causes an inevitable breakdown in communication and trust between staff and pupils.

RIGID CURRICULUM

Left to themselves, children have an insatiable thirst for knowledge and will learn things all the time. A school, however, sets a curriculum and tries to make children learn specific things at particular times.

This destroys the child's interest in learning.

RIGID TIMETABLE

Children do not like to be restrained or to have their time rigidly controlled. Left to themselves, they become absorbed in something for a while and then move on to something else.

By setting a timetable, schools try to switch a child's interest in various subjects on and off in a competely unnatural fashion. Since children are not clockwork machines they do not respond to this treatment. They just become tired and lose interest.

Any educational institution that does not force a rigid timetable and curriculum upon its pupils, and which all the children involved are willing to attend, will not suffer from all the problems that are associated with schools.

ALTERNATIVE SCHOOLS
The widespread dissatisfaction with schools has led to several attempts to establish new types of school. These include

FREE SCHOOLS
These vary greatly depending upon the adult staff involved. One source of problems in Free Schools is that adults in the school are so keen to avoid adopting authoritarian roles that they fail to give the children adequate direction.

Free Schools have to be judged as they are seen. They can work well for a while if the right mix of pupils and teachers come together.

RUDOLF STEINER SCHOOLS
These represent the largest category of Alternative Schools. Their educational approach is based upon the teaching of Rudolf Steiner, an Austrian philosopher. Although this approach has much to recommend it, the way in which it is applied tends to be inflexible,and the curriculum in these schools can be even more rigid than that of State Schools, and of little relevance to life in the modern world.

The idea of "Alternative Schools" is very attractive to many parents and teachers, and over the years many attempts have been made to establish schools that are kinder to children. Not many of them have stood the test of time, and many have been forced to close because the children involved have rebelled against the philosophy that was motivating the staff. The problem is that school is, by its nature, unfriendly to children, and to pretend otherwise is hypocritical.

Most children would prefer to go to a conventional school that they don't like than to an unconventional school that seems, to them, to be be equally pointless, and which isolates them from the rest of society.

Alternative Schools that have survived are often ones where the parents of the children who attend are united by a common religious or philosophical belief that causes them to override their children's objections to the education that they are receiving.

Of course, not all schools are bad. When a good teacher or group of teachers is able to work with a certain amount of freedom, then they may be able to create conditions in which children can prosper and receive a good education.

Such situations are rare, and parents should beware of deluding themselves into thinking that they have found such a school and committing their child to several wasted years of school attendance.

ADVANTAGES OF HOME EDUCATION

Most people who educate their children at home only do so after considering every other option, and often after having sent their children to school for many unhappy years.

They choose Home Education as a last resort but, in many ways, it is a form of education ideally suited to the changing circumstances of modern life. The advantages of Home Education are best appreciated through practical experience, but can be indicated as follows

STRENGTHENS THE FAMILY

Whether they live in a one-parent or two-parent family, children's main source of support is their family. Home Education makes a child feel more secure and able to trust their family for help and guidance through the difficult process of growing up.

EDUCATIONAL ADVANTAGES

A Home Educated child does not have to sit through hours of lessons which they don't understand (or find too easy). They therefore retain an interest in learning. They work at their own pace, covering much work at a greater depth than they could do in school.

MAKES THE CHILD MORE RESPONSIBLE

Schoolchildren are always being told what to do and, as a result, trying to find ways of not doing it. Freed from this pointless cycle, Home Educated children mature and take responsibility for their actions from a much younger age.

LESS INCLINED TO SWEAR, SMOKE, DRINK AND TAKE DRUGS

Removed from peer group pressures and the need to retain credibility amongst classmates, a Home Educated child does not have to swear, smoke, drink or take drugs in order to survive socially.

PREPARATION FOR LIFE

Only teachers go to to school when they grow up. Everyone else has to adapt to life in the outside world. A Home Educated child is already in the outside world, and is therefore ideally prepared to deal with it.

IT IS FUN

Parents who do not teach their children at home probably never realise what good company their children are, and miss their chance to be with their children while they are growing up.

Nothing is as much fun as working and learning with a child, and if that child is your own child and knows that you have chosen to look after him or her yourself instead of sending them off to school, then the pleasure that you will experience is unsurpassable.

WHAT TYPE OF CHILD IS HOME TAUGHT?

Nearly every parent has heard of Home Education but many think that it is only suitable for certain types of child. While this is not the case, it is true that some children just do not fit into the school system and, in effect, demand to be home educated. Some examples are

GIFTED CHILDREN

Some children appear to have an intellectual capacity far beyond the average. It is impossible for a school to meet the educational needs of such children, causing them either to switch off and become lethargic or else to vent their frustration through disruptive behaviour.

Some subjects such as Mathematics and Creative Writing call for the ability to think and reason in an unconventional manner. Aptitude in these areas can be stifled by early schooling.

Liberated from the repressive atmosphere of school, a gifted child will take responsibility for studying their chosen subject themselves and can make substantial progress without any specialist tutoring. A parent simply has to ensure that other areas are not neglected.

DYSLEXIC CHILDREN

The term "dyslexic" is applied to people who experience difficulty in reading and writing. In its present usage it does not refer to one particular sort of reading difficulty. Dyslexic people may get words and letters back to front, get letters jumbled up, have difficulty in identifying the different letters and putting them together to make words, and usually cannot see how spoken words can be represented as a series of letters. As a consequence, they experience serious problems with spelling, and often find the process of writing quite uncomfortable.

65

Apart from lacking the one skill of being unable to work with the written language, dyslexic people may be very gifted and be capable of achieving great success in a wide variety of careers and professions.

Unfortunately, school can be very hard on dyslexic children, as so much of the curriculum is centred around reading and writing. Dyslexic children are often classified as having "Special Educational Needs", and are subjected to years of pressure to try and make them do something of which they are almost incapable. Even when they do make progress in reading and writing, they feel inferior to other children who read and write with ease.

When educated at home, such children do not have to have a curriculum based upon reading and writing, and as a consequence do not grow up being made to feel that they are in some way mentally deficient.

MUSICAL CHILDREN

Some children have a particular love of music and desire to play a musical instrument. There is little opportunity to practise during the school day, and children who attend school have to fit their practice into evenings and weekends, which severely limits progress.

Children taught at home have much more time because they do not have to endure all the time-wasting that goes on in school and, of course, do not have to travel every day.

Specialist schools do exist for musical pupils, but the home can provide at least as good an education, particularly if a good tutor is available for regular tuition.

CHILDREN WITH SPECIAL NEEDS

Many children are designated as having "Special Educational Needs" (SEN). These include Down's Syndrome children, children who have suffered from brain damage, children who have a mental and emotional age much younger than their years and children who have chronic illnesses that have affected their development.

The Local Education Authority (LEA) is obliged to offer education for all these children whilst they are of "compulsory school age". The problem is that most of them are unlikely to make much progress in the conventional school curriculum.

Consequently most LEA's provide Special Schools which specifically cater for the needs of these children, and in which the children are often happy. Unfortunately, these schools cannot prepare their pupils for later life. The care and attention which the pupils become used to is abruptly withdrawn when they are sixteen, and they are expected to fend for themselves.

In order to avoid this trauma, most LEA's now try to incorporate children with special needs into mainstream schools and give them extra attention within those schools. Such children then get the worst of both worlds. They are never going to master the material in the school curriculum, but they have to endure all the indignities of life in school.

Home education is therefore a very attractive option for such children. Some children, depending upon their particular condition, can learn surprisingly well when intensively tutored by their parent and can actually make up ground on other children, and integrate into the system at a later stage.

Others, more severely disabled, simply find the home environment more secure, and are able to develop their interests in an atmosphere free from pressure and disruption.

The obvious drawback for parents is the amount of time and energy that children with special needs can demand. The task is made easier if parents receive practical support from friends and relatives. Possibly because of this difficulty, parents of children who are registered at a Special School may not withdraw them without the consent of the Local Authority.

67

While it is true that all the afore-mentioned groups do benefit from Home Education, categorising them in such a way implies that school is quite adequate for "normal" children. In fact, each child is unique and has their own special needs which can best be met in a loving home environment. The categories of children that benefit from Home Education could be extended as follows

YOUNG CHILDREN

The first day of school is a shocking experience for everyone. It is a memory that most people carry with them for the rest of their lives. Being left alone in a strange room, in a strange building, in the care of a stranger and having to follow a strange routine is very disturbing for a young child. Simple activities, such as going to the toilet or having a drink, become the source of great anxiety.  Public ridicule might ensue from not being able to do up one's shoelaces or wipe one's bottom properly. In addition, children feel a real loss at not being with their parents and their brothers and sisters, and cannot understand why they have to go to school.

Some children become hysterical during their first weeks at school, and have fits of uncontrollable screaming and shouting; others weep silently while others simply sit with a blank, dazed expression on their faces.

Eventually most children settle into a submissive acceptance of school, but this should not be seen as a positive sign - it shows that they have been hurt but cannot find a remedy. They make the best of a bad situation and harbour resentment against those who are responsible.

The fact that a child does not go to Primary School does not mean that they will never be able to fit into the system. It is quite common for

Home educated children to choose to go to Secondary
School for a variety of reasons - a desire to mix
with people of their own age, to get certain qualifications or just to see what school is like.
They generally have quite a good time at school
as they are there by choice, and have made up their
minds to put up with its shortcomings.

OLDER CHILDREN

Secondary Schools concentrate almost exclus-
ively on work for GCSE and A levels. Their success
is largely measured by how many children get five
or more GCSE's at Grade A,B or C (which should be
equivalent to the old 'O' level), and how many go
on to study for 'A' level.

More than sixty per cent of pupils fail to
get five GCSE's at Grade A,B or C and it is question-
able whether the qualifications with which they
leave school are of any use at all. They have every
reason to believe that their five years of Secondary
education are a waste of time,and that they would
be much better off learning practical skills, working
at home.

CHILDREN WHO UNDERACHIEVE AT SCHOOL

It is not only very gifted children who find
the pace of school work difficult to cope with.
The difficulty that many children experience in
Mathematics can usually be traced to some aspect
of their early schooling, and the same can often
be said for children with reading difficulties.

School is notorious for being able to make
exciting subjects tedious and objectionable. In
addition, an apparent failure in a subject at school
can leave children with an impression that lasts
for life,-that they are "no good" at Painting,
Drawing, Woodwork, French, History, Science etc.

If you are worried that your child is starting
to underachieve and to develop a poor self image,
then now is the time to consider taking them out
of school.

WHAT TYPE OF PARENT TEACHES AT HOME?

"QUALIFIED TEACHERS", PEOPLE WITH 'A'LEVELS AND DEGREES

The term "qualified teacher" is a little misleading as it usually means qualified to teach in school. The techniques used in school can be a real disadvantage if used at home. Children do not expect to be lectured or bossed around at home; they expect lessons to be conducted in a civilised manner.

"Qualified" teachers, therefore, have to rethink their approach radically, but having done so can teach their own children very effectively. In fact, many Home Educators are qualified teachers. This may be because they have confidence in their own ability, but is probably also due to the fact that, having recent first-hand knowledge of schools, they are reluctant to subject their own children to school conditions.

PEOPLE WITH NO ACADEMIC QUALIFICATIONS

People with no academic qualifications often doubt their ability to teach. This is a pity because they have certain distinct advantages.

In the first place, having been to school for up to eleven years themselves with nothing to show for it, they will be acutely aware of how schools go wrong, and will be able to avoid making the same mistakes themselves.

Secondly, they will be sympathetic to difficulties that their children experience in learning, and will be able to help them resolve them. People who become very expert in a subject often lose their ability to communicate their knowledge to others on a simple level.

Thirdly, parents who did not do well at school themselves, become just as excited as their children by the material being studied, as they have never really taken it in before. It is very inspiring for a child to feel that their parent is really interested in work that they are doing.

It is worth remembering that parents with absolutely no academic qualifications are just as legally entitled to teach their own children as anyone else.

SINGLE PARENTS

Many single parents do educate their children at home, but they suffer from the obvious difficulty of not having income from a full-time job coming into the home, as well. Some people have tried to resolve this by communal living. They share responsibility for caring for and educating their children between several families, so that some of the parents can go out to work. Others have supportive families in which the children's grandparents are pleased to participate, while others just choose to live on a very low income so that they can teach their children at home.

TWO PARENT FAMILIES

Where there are two parents in the family it is usually possible to manage with only one parent going out to work. However, the parent who goes to work may feel that they are missing out on a rather wonderful experience.

There is also an increasing amount of Home-based employment, and where this is available life obviously becomes easier for the Home Educating family.

LEGAL ASPECTS OF HOME EDUCATION

The following few pages outline the main legal aspects of Home Education. They are not intended to cover every possible circumstance, but do provide sufficient information to meet the needs of most parents. If you find yourself in a particularly difficult or complicated legal situation then you should seek expert advice - initially from Education Otherwise (see address list).

The parents' right to educate their children out of school is clearly stated in the 1944 Education Act.

"It shall be the duty of the parent of every child of compulsory school age to cause him to receive efficient full time education suitable to his age, ability and aptitude and to any special educational needs he may have, either by regular attendance at school or otherwise."

- from the 1944 Education Act (as amended by the 1981 Education Act)

It seems unlikely this "otherwise" option was originally intended for the use of ordinary people, but over the past forty years a succession of court cases have clearly established the right of parents to educate their children, irrespective of their own educational background and qualifications.

It has become the responsibility of the Local Education Authority to ensure that parents who do not send their child to school do provide them with an education.

THE LOCAL EDUCATION AUTHORITY

If a Home Educating family has any contact with the Educational establishment, then it will be through the Local Education Authority (LEA). The policies and procedures of LEAs vary in different parts of the country, and it is a good idea to get in touch with other Home Educating families in your area (via Education Otherwise) in order to become familiar with the attitude of your local LEA.

At the present time, Home Educators are not a very significant factor in the life of the LEA s and, providing a home educating family does not go out of its way to antagonise the LEA, they should not expect to be unduly disturbed.

The route by which a family arrives at the decision to home educate determines the initial relationship with the LEA.

CHILDREN WHO HAVE NEVER BEEN TO A STATE-FUNDED SCHOOL

If you start home educating as soon as your child is of compulsory school age, or if you withdraw your child from an Independent School, then you need not inform the LEA at all.

The LEA is obliged to take action if it thinks that a child is not receiving an education "suitable to their age, ability and aptitude". Whilst the fact that a child is home educated is not in itself reason to supose that the education is inadequate, most LEA's choose to interpret the law as obliging them to ensure that the education is suitable, by arranging for an Educational Advisor to visit, when they become aware that a child is being home educated.

This may be offensive to some families, but most prefer to cooperate rather than become involved in legal arguments that could distract them from what they really want to do i.e. educate their child.

Some parents decide to inform the LEA that

73

they are educating their child at home, rather than
wait for them to find out in some other way.

AUTOMATIC DEREGISTRATION
Even when your child is registered at a State-
funded school, there are certain circumstances that
allow them to be automatically deregistered. The
most common of these are

- when a child has completed Primary or Middle
  School education and you have not yet
  accepted a place in a Secondary School.

- when you move out of the area covered by
  your LEA.

- when you move within the area of your LEA
  but too far from your child's present school
  for commuting to be practical.

- if you go to live abroad for a short while
  and then return home.

- if your child is permanently excluded
  (expelled) from school.

If your child is automatically deregistered,
then your legal position is the same as that just
discussed for parents whose children have never
been to a State-funded school.

WITHDRAWING YOUR CHILD FROM SCHOOL WITH THE
CO-OPERATION OF THE HEAD TEACHER
If your child is attending a State funded
school, and you wish to withdraw them, then you
have to ask the Head Teacher to remove your child's
name from the register. This is best done at the
end of term to minimise disruption to your child's
class. The request should be made in writing, and
you should state your intention to Home Educate.
LEA schools are not meant to deregister pupils
until they are convinced that adequate alternative

education has been arranged. Most Head Teachers, however, will comply with a reasonable request, but they will also inform the LEA of your action, so that in these circumstances you must expect fairly early contact from an Education Adviser.

WITHDRAWING YOUR CHILD FROM SCHOOL WITHOUT THE CO-OPERATION OF THE HEADTEACHER

Sometimes a certain amount of conflict develops when parents inform a Head Teacher of their decision to Home Educate. This may be due to the rather narrow view that some teachers hold that children can only be educated properly in school, or it may be due to the fact that the child is being withdrawn from school because the relationship between school and the child has broken down.

Children who may otherwise be good-natured can be driven to disruptive and aggressive behaviour by being made to go to school. They can also become chronically ill, leading to long and repeated periods of absence or irregular attendance. When such a pattern starts to develop, both the child and their family become labelled as being "a problem". A request to deregister a child in such circumstances may not be met favourably, and the Head Teacher may refuse.

To complicate matters further, when a child has been very disturbed by school it is difficult to initiate a programme of Home Education. The child is too mixed up to dive into something new with enthusiasm. This makes it impossible for the parent to prove that they have made adequate educational provision to replace school.

If you find yourself in this situation you should

- contact Education Otherwise for advice (see address list)

- write to the Head Teacher requesting that your child be deregistered from a certain date - preferably the end of term or half term.

- outline in your letter the reason for your action. Explain the ways in which you feel that your child is not receiving an education "suitable to his age, ability and aptitude" at school, and state that you will be providing this sort of education at home.

- withdraw your child from school

- prepare yourself for a visit from an Education Adviser (do not allow yourself to become involved in disputes with Educational Social Workers whose job it is to persuade truants to return to school).

When you have removed your child from school you may find that LEA officials are more sympathetic. "Difficult" children take up a disproportionate amount of scarce resources, and persistent truants spoil a school's attendance statistics. Once the LEA is convinced that you are serious in your intention to educate your child, it may be grateful that you have relieved them of a problem.

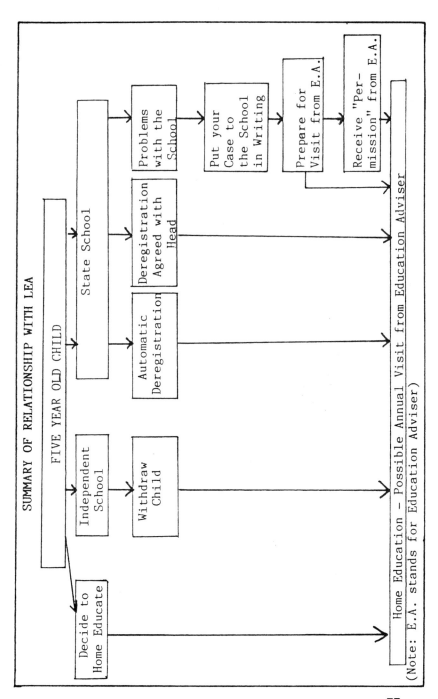

SUMMARY OF RELATIONSHIP WITH LEA

FIVE YEAR OLD CHILD

Decide to Home Educate

Independent School

State School

Withdraw Child

Automatic Deregistration

Deregistration Agreed with Head

Problems with the School

Put your Case to the School in Writing

Prepare for Visit from E.A.

Receive "Permission" from E.A.

Home Education – Possible Annual Visit from Education Adviser

(Note: E.A. stands for Education Adviser)

77

EDUCATION ADVISERS

WHAT IS AN EDUCATION ADVISER?
LEA's employ Education Advisers to monitor their schools. The Adviser will either specialise in a particular age group (Primary, Secondary etc.); or in a subject (Maths, Reading etc.). They are teachers who have chosen to give up their classroom teaching role in favour of being an Adviser.

Education Advisers are not to be confused with Educational Social Workers/Educational Welfare Officers who have no teaching experience, and whose job it is to persuade truants to return to school. Home Educating families usually prefer to have no dealings with Educational Social Workers.

WHOM DO THEY VISIT?
Most Home Educating families will, at some time, receive a request from their LEA that an Education Adviser should be allowed to visit.

This will certainly be the case for a child who has been withdrawn from a State School, as the LEA is then obliged to ensure that the child is receiving an adequate education. An Adviser is also likely to wish to visit parents who write to inform the LEA of their decision to home educate.

Most LEA's ask their Advisers to return once a year to Home Educating families on their lists.

WHAT DO THEY OFFER?
Not being experienced in Home Education, and not having any resources at their disposal, Education Advisers have little to offer Home Educating families

WHAT ARE THE DANGERS?
There is always an element of danger when dealing with a bureaucracy. Nine out of ten Advisers may be perfectly reasonable, and supportive of Home Educating families. The tenth may be a dyed in the wool traditionalist with an unshakeable belief

in the worth of schools and a mistrust of anyone who steps out of line.

In such situations parents have much more at stake than the Adviser. The peace and tranquillity of their lives can be shattered if they start to receive letters from an LEA making suggestions and demanding action.

The present situation of LEA's sending their School Advisers to Home Educating families is unsatisfactory. If the LEA really believes that it has a duty to monitor Home Educating families, then it should employ Advisers with experience of Home Education. However, there is no prospect of imminent change, and families have to be prepared to cope with the system as it is.

HOW TO CONDUCT THE INTERVIEW
When an Adviser visits
    —make it plain that you are a member of Education Otherwise (if you are!). This is a fairly small organisation, but it is nationwide, and has successfully represented many Home Educating families. An official will feel less inclined to throw his or her weight around if they think that they are up against a national organisation.

    - listen carefully to what they have to say, and make notes.

    - prepare a clear description of the education that you are providing and explain it clearly and concisely.

    - do not try to convince the Adviser— they make their living in the School system. Do not be defensive about what you are doing.

    - have a friend present to give you moral support.

    - ask for a copy of any report that they write.

79

- keep a file of all correspondence with the LEA.

- have everything that you will need for the interview, to hand.

- be careful about allowing an adviser to question your children. It is very difficult for anyone to judge a child's state of mind or educational progress from a short interview, so don't give them a chance to form the wrong impression.

WHAT ARE YOU REQUIRED TO PROVE?
Your main duty as a Home Educating parent is to be able to demonstrate that your child is receiving an "efficient full-time education suitable to his age, ability and aptitude."
The following definitions may help to clarify this phrase.

FULL-TIME

Full-time education is not the same as a full-time job. State schools are open for about thirty-nine weeks of the year, and Independent schools far less. Schoolchildren are at school between about 9.00 a.m. and 3.45 p.m.
Pupils that receive private tuition do not need such long hours (and could not cope with them), to cover the same amount of work. The maximum number of hours of home tuition that an LEA will provide for children who are off school, is two hours per day. This is deemed to meet the requirement of full-time education.
When a parent is Home Educating then education probably really is full-time. Certain times of the day may be allocated to formal lessons, but the communication between adult and child, which is the real basis of education, continues throughout the day.

EDUCATION SUITABLE TO AGE, APTITUDE AND ABILITY
This is clearly very difficult to define, as who can say what aptitude and ability a particular child has?

The term "education" implies some form of systematic instruction, and a parent who does have formal lessons with their child will find it easier to convince an official that education is taking place than someone who doesn't. However, parents who have just arranged practical activities for their children, with no academic work, have successfully argued that they are providing an education.

EFFICIENT
This is probably the most contentious term as it implies that the education given meets its objectives. This is clearly not the case for the majority of Secondary Schools whose aim is for their pupils to attain high levels of GCSE passes.

Home Educators, on the other hand, may have different objectives, and it is not possible to tell whether these objectives have been attained until a child has grown up and put what he or she has learnt into practice.

TIMETABLE AND CURRICULUM
A school cannot function without a timetable and, nowadays, also needs a detailed curriculum. Section 3 of this book discusses the relevance of timetables and curricula to the process of Home Education. Many families find them to be artificial and restrictive, and rapidly dispense with them.

An Adviser, however, whose sole education experience is of a school, may find it difficult to envisage any system not based upon a timetable and curriculum. It is common for the LEA to ask for a copy of your timetable and curriculum.

If this happens, you may feel that the simplest course is to comply with the request. If so, you can either try to structure your child's week in a rigid timetable or else you can make a list of all the activities that you do with your child, and arrange them in the form of a typical week,

which you can then present as your timetable.
For example

	MON.	TUES.	WED.	THUR.	FRI.
9-11 11.15-1	ENGLISH MATHS	HISTORY FRENCH	MATHS ENGLISH	etc.	
2-3.30	ART	MUSIC	GAMES	etc.	

In the same way, you can list all the different
"subjects" that you cover, and state what you hope
to achieve over the coming year.

READING - Developing reading skills in line with aptitude and inclination.

WRITING - Practise joined up writing learnt last year.

ARITHMETIC - Tables. Addition and subtraction.

etc.

You can be as specific or as vague as you
wish, and you must remember that you are not obliged
to cover the same areas as the National Curriculum.

The danger is that once you produce these
sorts of documents, you are open to being given
advice about how to make improvements. These pieces
of paper are filed away and brought out the following
year for comparison. Instead of arguing your case
on the basis of principles that you believe in,
and make sense, you have allowed the argument to
be shifted onto ground on which the School Adviser
feels comfortable.

You may therefore prefer not to supply a written timetable and curriculum. If this is the case, then you must be prepared to demonstrate to the Adviser the kind of work that you are doing, and that you are providing a good education for your child.

Collect all the written work that your child has done, any Maths or Arithmetic, all the pictures that they have painted or drawn and things that they have made. Show this work to the Adviser and explain carefully how it was done, and why you teach the subjects that you do. If your child has difficulty with Reading or Arithmetic, explain this as well so that the Adviser does not form the impression that you are neglecting these areas.

Make notes of your discussions with the Adviser and keep them in a file. When the Adviser calls again, the following year, repeat the process, pointing out all the things that have been done since the last visit.

In this way you are demonstrating what you have achieved, and are not having to make guesses or promises about what you might achieve.

In the long run this is much less stressful to you, as you are in control of the situation.

ADVICE FROM THE ADVISER

The Adviser may give advice out of habit because s/he thinks that that is her/his job. A Home Educating family does not have to follow the National Curiculum, but on the other hand does not want to antagonise the Adviser.

Advice should therefore be listened to politely and considered carefully. If you decide not to accept it then politely point out that you intend to cover the proposed subject (Science, Languages etc.) in some other way or at a later date. Do not not promise to do something that you have no intention of doing.

LETTING THE ADVISER TALK TO YOUR CHILDREN

The Adviser may assume that they have a right to talk to your children and question them about their education.

You do not have to allow this to happen.

You are the person responsible for the child's education and it is to you that the Adviser should look for information about this education. It is not their job to assess the educational progress of your child or to question them on their attitude to school.

You may decide to let the Adviser speak to your child in order to avoid any suspicion that you have something to hide. If you do so then you must remember that the Adviser is the product of a School system that does not treat children with respect or courtesy, and your child should be warned what to expect.

If you feel that the Adviser oversteps the limit of acceptable questions then you may have to intervene. However, where possible, you should try to conduct an interview with the Adviser in as civil a manner as possible, as there is nothing to be gained by provoking unnecessary confrontation with the LEA.

SETTING UP YOUR OWN SCHOOL

If you find that you are in a situation where you are teaching several children who do not go to school, then you may wish to register as an Independent School.

HOW DO YOU REGISTER?

If you provide full-time education for five or more children of compulsory school age (including your own children), then you should write to the Department of Education and Science (DES) and become provisionally registered as an Independent School (see address list).

FIRE REGULATIONS

The DES will then contact your local Fire Service and a Fire Safety Officer will come and check your premises for safety. S/he will make recommendations about having adequate exits, extinguishers and fire blankets, with which you must comply. If you are only teaching half a dozen or so children then these requirements will not be much more strict than the precautions that you take in your own home.

HER MAJESTY'S INSPECTOR OF SCHOOLS (HMI)

You will then be contacted by an HMI, who will come and visit you usually two or three months after your initial application. You must explain the ethos of your "school", and provide a copy of a curriculum on this visit.

The HMI s are, amongst other things, responsible for monitoring Independent Schools. These are much more diverse than State Schools. They range from Free Schools on the one hand to Public Schools on the other. The HMI will, therefore, be more broad-minded than the average LEA Adviser, and will not necessarily be expecting you to follow the National Curriculum.

You have to demonstrate to the HMI that you know what you are doing, that you provide good supervision for the children in your care and that you are giving the children an opportunity to acquire a good general education.

The Inspector will try and approve a School whenever possible and if a school falls below an acceptable standard, will suggest improvements rather than give an outright refusal to approve registration.

PLANNING PERMISSION

If you are planning to use premises other than your home, or if you need to make structural alterations in order to operate as a School, then you will need planning permission, which may be difficult.

Although most people send their children to school, no-one wants to live next to one. People assume that all schoolchildren are noisy and a nuisance, and are likely to oppose planning permission in residential areas.

PRIVATE TUITION

If the process sounds too daunting, but you still wish to teach children who don't go to school, then you can consider doing so as a private tutor.

In this case each parent must account to their LEA for the education that their child is receiving, and explain that they are using you as a private tutor.

RECOVERING FROM SCHOOL

THE PROBLEM
If your child has been attending school for a long period of time, then you cannot expect to start Home Education without a period of adjustment.

Pupils in school develop two types of reaction to lessons.

AGGRESSION
Sometimes they feel very hostile and antagonistic towards the school, the teacher, the subject and the material that they are being taught.

PASSIVITY
More commonly, pupils develop a submissive acceptance of lessons, and stop expecting to learn very much or have an interesting time.

When they are removed from school, children retain this mixture of aggression and disinterest towards anything that resembles schoolwork.

Some children develop very extreme reactions to specific subjects (such as Maths), and trying to introduce these into the home can provoke violent reactions of fear, anger and depression.

TELEVISION, COMPUTER GAMES AND LOUD MUSIC
Children who attend school are under considerable stress. They have very little freedom of choice during their day and are forced to attend lessons that leave them drained or exhausted.

When they come home from school, they are often not in the mood for constructive activity (such as playing, drawing, reading, practising a musical instrument, studying etc.). They tend, instead, to abandon themselves to something that requires little effort on their part such as watching television, playing computer games or listening to loud music.

A child, removed from school, with no experi-

ence of managing their own time, will be inclined
to fill their whole day with this sort of activity.

THE SOLUTION
In such circumstances a parent must exercise
self-restraint and allow the healing effect of time
to bring about a cure. After a few weeks or months
the inexhaustible curiosity and desire for fresh
knowledge that every human being is born with, will
begin to reassert itself in your child.

WALKING AND TALKING
The outdoors has a beneficial effect on everyone and is particularly liberating to a child who
has been cooped up in a school. Children often
find it easier to talk about their feelings and
experiences when they are walking or engaged in
some other activity, as they do not then feel pressurised. They feel able to tell you about the in-
cidents and people that made their time at school
painful or unbearable.
The more of your undivided attention that
you can give to your child at this time, the quicker
your relationship will be restored to its proper
strength. Going for long walks, every day if necessary, is a good way of achieving this.

INTRODUCING "LESSONS"
Some children retain a strong interest in
some subjects throughout their time at school, indeed
they may be frustrated that they cannot spend more
time on them. Such subjects can be studied to the
child's satisfaction from the time that they leave
school.
For children without such an interest, and
who have been disturbed by the routine of school,
it is a good idea to encourage them to help in activities such as cooking, gardening, cleaning, shopping,
woodworking, decorating, craftwork, modelling etc.
These activities are useful, do not have the painful
association of "lessons" and help to build up a
pattern of making good use of time.
It is then relatively easy to introduce reading
and writing based subjects in due course.

SECTION III

EDUCATING YOUR CHILD AT HOME

GETTING STARTED

The previous sections outline the disadvantages of school and how you can extricate your child from school once you have made up your mind to do so.

You now have to decide how you are to go about educating your child at home. The main advantage is that you have the freedom to adopt a style and method that suits you and your child, you do not have to adhere to an externally imposed regime.

The following pages give some suggestions and outline some of the techniques that have worked for other children.

One of the biggest problems that parents face is that, in their own minds, school and education are inseparable, and they therefore feel that they have to have their children sitting and working for several hours per day in order to teach them properly. This is not necessarily the case, and many children prefer to learn in other ways.

Initially you have to decide what to teach and when to teach it. The secret of success in Home Education is having a good communication with your child.

If you decide to introduce a subject to your child, but find that they cannot understand it, then you can leave it and try again at a later date.

On the other hand, if your child becomes particularly interested in something, then you can concentrate upon that for a while, knowing you can catch up on other work later.

Even so, you may wish to know what sort of work is being done in schools, and to have certain aims for each forthcoming year. If so, you can consult published school curricula.

NATIONAL CURRICULUM

The National Curriculum has been written by educationalists working in the State sector of education, and it outlines a programme of work that all State Schools must now follow.

It has been based upon the assumption that an "average" child will be ready to absorb a certain type of learning during each year of their schooling, and then goes on to impose this average on all children. The concept of a National Curriculum being forced upon all children causes much anxiety amongst many parents and teachers. However, it does provide a useful yardstick against which to measure the progress of your child, and it gives you a clear picture of what other children of their age are doing at school.

Simplified versions of the National Curriculum are available from bookshops.

RUDOLF STEINER CURRICULUM

Rudolf Steiner was an Austrian philosopher who lived at the beginning of this century. He had a great deal of teaching experience, gained through lecturing at Adult Education programmes and through being the private tutor of a handicapped boy (who subsequently went to University). Towards the end of his life he founded a school and drew upon his experience and insight to make suggestions about the curriculum.

This curriculum is used, to a certain extent, in Rudolf Steiner schools today and contains many ideas that Home Educating parents may find useful. Rudolf Steiner appears to have been a sensitive and caring teacher, much loved by his pupils, and his curriculum was devised to meet the mental, emotional and spiritual needs of children. This contrasts with the National Curriculum which been written by committees made up of people representing a variety of different interests.

TIMETABLE

The other thing that you must consider is your timetable. This does not mean having a set sequence of lessons each day, but rather that you establish a certain pattern to your week.

Children do like to have a routine, as it gives them security and a structure about which to organise themselves.

Your timetable will depend on how many children you are teaching at home and how many other essential activities you have to fit into your day.

The more of your undivided attention that you are able to give to your children, the more enjoyable and the more successful your experience of Home Education will be.

Ideally, any written work or work that requires intense concentration should be done in the morning. Artistic, Craft and Practical work can be done later in the day.

Once you establish a routine, you will find that there are times when you are working closely with your children, and then times when they are working, practising, reading, finishing off work or playing on their own.

Overall, you should find your existence to be considerably less stressful than if they were going to school.

FORMAL LESSONS

If you are having formal lessons then you will probably find that one or two hours per child per day of book work is as much as they can cope with - although they may wish to write and read on their own as well.

Older children, studying for exams, will need to work longer hours, but not necessarily with tuition.

AUTONOMOUS LEARNING

This is a popular phrase in the Home Education world and refers to the fact that children will always learn on their own, particularly if they are not pressurised to learn through formal in-struction.

This is especially true of older children and people in their teens who develop quite a strong resistance to being instructed formally in one subject after another. This fact should be very comforting to parents who know that they can help their child to read and write, but doubt their ability to proceed further.

Autonomous learning does not necessarily mean learning independently of the parent. Children will always enjoy discussing their reading material and their ideas with their parents if they know that their parents are interested, open-minded and are prepared to make sufficient time available for them.

YOUR TEACHING TECHNIQUE

This is obviously a very personal matter, and depends upon the relationship that you have with your child.

However, in general, you will be aiming somewhere in between formal lessons and autonomous learning. The idea of lecturing your child on certain subjects soon becomes ridiculous, but you cannot expect a child to know what subjects are interesting or worthy of study. Your role is therefore one of guiding your child in certain directions and making resources available. You can also work with your child, making suggestions and discussing the subject as you do so.

In subjects that do require a definite skill, such as Reading, Writing and Arithmetic, you will have to give clear instruction, and in every area you can give praise and encouragement. As the parent and teacher you have to be sensitive to your child's state of mind and be aware as to whether they have sufficient challenges or are over-stressed, and react accordingly.

RESOURCES

BOOKS
Books are undoubtedly the biggest single asset to Home Educating families. It is the relative cheapness and diversity of books that makes Home Education possible for most people.

Schools limit the number of books that they make available to children because books deteriorate rapidly in a school environment.

At home, children tend to treat their books with the respect that they deserve, and Home Educating families find the purchase of books to be a very worthwhile investment.

Second-hand book shops, Charity shops and jumble sales can prove to be a treasure trove of cheap books, both fiction and non-fiction.

Educational books are usually available in paperback and are quite reasonably priced. Bookshops contain a surprisingly diverse and interesting range of books covering all the subjects taught in school, often in a much more entertaining way than you would imagine.

Even with all the modern technological advances books remain the principal source of educational material. If you can surround your children with books, then you are giving them the opportunity to broaden their minds and develop their interests at their own pace and free from the pressure to work to an externally determined pattern.

LIBRARIES
Libraries can prove to be an excellent supplement to books that you have in the home.

Some Local Education Authorities allow Home Educating families to use their resource libraries (from which schools borrow books). This is a very useful facility which you should take advantage of if it is available in your area.

If it is not available, it is still possible

for a family to withdraw a substantial number of books, between them, from local libraries, and therefore to have a large pool of books constantly available to read and browse through.

Many areas are served by a Mobile Library, which calls on a weekday. The librarians are usually very pleased to help Home Educated children, on their round, to obtain the books that they need.

MUSEUMS, HISTORICAL BUILDINGS, WILDLIFE PARKS

Museums can be visited when they are relatively quiet during the week, when other children are at school. Education Otherwise has arranged free entry or entrance at a reduced rate for Home Educating families in several museums. Many other museums will offer a concession equivalent to that available to schools if you explain that you educate your children at home. The latter also applies to some Wildlife Parks and other establishments that are regularly visited by schoolchildren, but it is wise to phone and check the day before you intend to go.

TELEVISION AND RADIO

Television has to be treated with caution as an aid to education, as it forces a passive and non-participating role upon the viewer. There are, however, some programmes that may stimulate thought and open up new perspectives. Children often find wildlife programmes fascinating as they provide a chance to see plants and animals in their natural state.

Some of the Schools/Open University programmes can be useful, for example Modern Language programmes when used in connection with the Course book, offer a very good introduction to a new language.

FRIENDS AND RELATIONS

It may be that you have many friends and relations, old and young, who, when they begin to see the potential of Home Education, decide to offer your children some of their time and skill. They may have particular skills, interests or specialist knowledge which they are prepared to make available.

COMPUTERS

Personal computers have come down in price to such an extent that most families can now afford to purchase one if they so wish.

Opinions vary as to how useful a tool they are in education. You will have to decide whether a computer can make a positive contribution to your child's education and, if so, to what extent they should be encouraged to use it.

THE HOME

In many ways a happy family life within the home is the most valuable resource available to you when you home educate.

Most of the skills required in everyday life are brought into play in the home – from cooking and cleaning on the one hand, to carpentry, gardening and property maintenance on the other.

In the course of daily life, children encounter a wide variety of situations and people which stimulate them to learn and develop in a natural and harmonious manner.

EDUCATION OTHERWISE

In the 1970's, parents teaching their children at home decided that they would be in a stronger position if they formed a support group. They named it Education Otherwise after the phrase in the 1944 Education Act that allowed home education to continue.

Although the group has no full-time, paid officers, it is now a nationwide organisation capable of giving worthwhile support to any family wanting to educate their children at home.

It is particularly effective in giving good legal advice and helping parents in their dealings with the Local Authority. Most local authorities will take a family much more seriously if it becomes apparent that they are members of Education Otherwise.

Education Otherwise is a support group made up of home educating families. Activities that it organises in any particular area depends completely upon the members in that locality, and accordingly vary from place to place. You would have to contact your local coordinator (see address list at back of book), to find out what was happening in your area, or if you wanted practical support from Education Otherwise.

Some parents find E.O. a useful source of social contact for their children – enabling them to meet and play with other home educated children.

TEACHING YOUR CHILD TO READ

The educational needs of young children are quite different from those of older children. The main purpose of the first few years of education is to acquire the basic skills of Reading, Writing and Arithmetic. The following few pages provide a few suggestions for parents who are uncertain as to how to approach these subjects.

WHEN IS THE BEST TIME TO LEARN?
There is an assumption in this country that the younger children are when they learn to read the better off they will be in life.

In some areas this has led to the absurd situation where Infant Schools expect children to be able to read when they join at the age of five – almost negating the purpose of sending the child to school in the first place.

The National Curriculum sets out objectives for Reading for each age group and, over the years, tests have been developed that describe a child as having a Reading Age of 5, 7, 10, 12 etc. These ideas accept that some children will be further advanced than the "average" targets and assessments, and therefore that some children will fall behind them.

This has the unfortunate effect of making both the children and their parents feel inadequate and backward,and can lead to permanent problems in the child's educational development.

In complete contrast to the accepted practice, the Rudolf Steiner curriculum (in common with many European schools) does not attempt to teach reading until a child is seven years old. Some children find this frustrating and want to learn earlier, others still feel pressured by being by being made to read at this age but, on average, pupils in Steiner schools leave school being able to read at least as well as their counterparts in other schools.

Thus it is not the case that being able to read when very young confers an automatic advantage, since children who learn later may develop a stronger and more permanent interest in reading. Each child is different and, when taught at home, can be treated as an individual.

THE BEST TIME IS WHEN THE CHILD WANTS TO LEARN

Young children go through phases of being interested in reading. As a parent you can respond at these times and help them with letters and words.

Typically, the child will then lose interest for a few days, weeks or months and will become distressed and cross if you try to force them to read and write. Interest will then return and they will want to learn a bit more. Eventually it will all fit into place and they will be able to read.

PROBLEMS

Problems in this process are most likely to arise if a child is made to read and write when they are not interested and, as a result, becomes antagonistic or feels themselves to be a failure.

Some children experience real difficulty with reading and writing, and early pressure is more likely to make the problem worse rather than better.

READ TO YOUR CHILDREN

The one thing that is most likely to make a child learn to read is being read to. Children who develop a love of books and stories in their earliest years will naturally want to read for themselves when they get older.

TEACHING YOUR CHILD TO WRITE

One of the advantages of not teaching your child to read when they are very young is that you then have the chance to teach Reading and Writing at the same time.

Children who learn to write at the same time as they learn to read have a much greater awareness of spelling, punctuation and sentence structure.

CAPITAL LETTERS

Young children have small hands and are still learning to control their movements. They cannot, therefore, write properly with pens and pencils, and if they are encouraged to do so, produce untidy work and develop bad habits which they find difficult to lose later.

Up until the age of about seven it is better for them to work with thick wax crayons and to write in capitals. They learn to write simple messages such as TO MUMMY. I LOVE YOU (which is usually all they want to write). This teaches them to put spaces between words, to use full stops, to spell words correctly and to write the letters the correct way round.

Children of this age also love to learn the alphabet. You can introduce one letter per day in the form of a story and then draw a picture to go with it, making up a personal Alphabet Book.

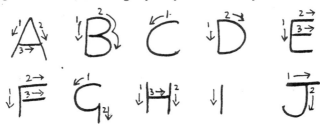

MAKING BOOKS

Simple books that you or your child write yourselves are often an easier introduction to reading than printed books. The stories can be very simple, related to everyday events in the child's life and the writing is in capital letters.

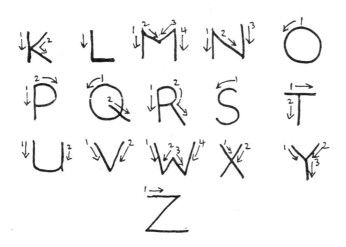

PRINTING

Once a child has learnt to read capital letters it is surprising how quickly they will pick up learning to read printed material.

You can go through the alphabet again showing the lower case (small) letter that goes with each capital, and can then go back over very simple books that you read to your child when they were much younger, and which they probably know almost by heart. Once they get the hang of these, they will quickly move on to books that they find interesting.

There is no need to teach a child to write in printing — it is not a skill that they will need when they grow up and it is really a waste of the child's time and effort. It is better to proceed to a style of joined-up writing that you find attractive and serviceable, and which you yourself are prepared to use.

JOINED-UP WRITING

If your child is working with you then they will want to be able to copy and read your handwriting. You will, therefore, have to practise a style of writing that you would like them to learn, and then use it consistently. An example of the Cursive script is given below.

Children can usually hold a pencil and produce attractive joined-up writing by the time they are about seven.

Start with simple exercises and build up to words when they have mastered the skill of writing the letters in various combinations. When an easy, flowing style has been achieved with a pencil, a fountain pen can be used. Biros should be left until the child is older.

Cursive script

a b c d e f
g h i j k
l m n o p q
r s t u v w x
y z abcdefghij
klmnopqrstuv
wxyz
A B C D
E F G H I J
K L M N O
P Q R S T
U V W X Y
Z

103

ARITHMETIC

Arithmetic and Mathematics are really two quite different subjects, and being good at one does not necessarily make one good at the other. Of the two, Arithmetic is by far the most useful to the majority of people, as it deals with numbers.

The following pages give some ideas about how to teach Arithmetic, and try to allay any of the fears that parents may have in this area.

MENTAL ARITHMETIC

Children love to count from an early age and this should be encouraged. When they get older they like to answer questions such as "What is two and two?" Numbers have a great fascination.

Some children work out the answer to questions such as "three add four" on their fingers or by counting pebbles, conkers etc. Whilst this is alright, the ultimate aim of Mental Arithmetic is to enable children instantly to know that the answer is seven — to acquire a feel for the right answer. This is done by repeated practice —not in a threatening manner but in such a way as to make it appear to be a sort of game.

In this way children acquire a knowledge of addition and subtraction and the beginnings of the multiplication tables before they learn to write numbers down.

Mental Arithmetic should be continued throughout education, with the questions becoming more challenging. Problems such as estimating the total bill whilst doing the shopping in the Supermarket, and comparing the estimate to the actual cost, are very useful exercises. Mental Arithmetic challenges the mind to think in a way that other subjects cannot imitate.

CALCULATORS

Young children who regularly use calculators often find it impossible to develop the ability to do Mental Arithemtic - it is too easy just to press the butons and read the answer on the display. It is therefore better not to provide them with a calculator but to help them to develop their basic skills in Arithmetic in the conventional way, and then let them use a calculator as an aid to working out more complex problems when they are older. In this way your child's abilities will be enhanced, not restricted, by the use of a machine.

WRITTEN ARITHMETIC

When a child starts to write letters they will also want to write numbers. It does no harm to treat them with the same respect and to have a book of numbers similar to the Alphabet book.
Children often write numbers the wrong way round, and spending time talking about the actual shapes of the figures can therefore be quite worthwhile.

SUMS

Very few children feel pleased or motivated when they find that they get sums wrong.

In Mental Arithmetic they don't mind having a guess, being wrong, and trying again, but a series of crosses on a page convinces them that Arithmetic is too hard, and that they cannot do it.

Written sums should therefore, initially, be used to reinforce skills already acquired in mental Arithmetic, so that the child can expect to get most of them right.

If you stick to the principle of only setting sums that you know the child can do, because you have discussed them and worked lots of examples together, then you will find that your child will look forward to, and enjoy, sessions of Arithmetic.

The usual order for covering Arithmetic is addition, subtraction, multiplication tables, simple multiplication, "short" division, long multiplication and long division.

PARENTAL FEARS

Mathematics is the subject that causes most problems in schools, and which leaves the most people with a sense of inadequacy. It is the one subject that causes parents to doubt their ability to Home Educate. Few people, however, find that they are as incompetent as they imagine themselves to be, once they start teaching their children.

Many people learn or relearn the tables for themselves whilst teaching, and find the increased work on Mental Arithmetic very stimulating and rewarding.

Apart from the basic number work already described, the only areas that really must be covered are fractions, money, weight, measurement and decimals.

FRACTIONS

Fractions make sense in a way that decimals do not. Everyone understands the meaning of a half or a quarter, whilst the idea of 0·5 or 0·25 does not have the same resonance.

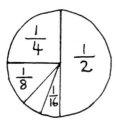

At one time, fractions had many more practical applications in everyday life than they do now.

Both Feet and Inches and Pounds and Ounces make use of fractions – quarter of a pound, eighth of an inch etc., but Metric measurements do not.

If you can teach your child to add, subtract, multiply and divide in fractions then you are laying the groundwork for a study of Algebra and Mathematics. If you cannot do this, then you need not reproach yourself as few schoolchildren are competent in this area. Young people can learn fractions on their own if they decide to study for a GCSE later on.

MONEY

The concept of decimals is quite difficult to understand from a mathematical viewpoint, but the idea of money is easy because it plays such an important role in everyday life.

You can teach children about money as and when they want to learn. Start with the value of coins and notes, and then begin to work things out mentally   and on paper.   Children enjoy counting money, and as they get older you can involve your child in any monetary calculations that you have to do yourself, such as checking the Electricity bill or the Bank statement.

Any mathematical problem that is drawn from your real life is going to have much greater significance to your child, and ideally you should set very few made-up problems in the early years of your child's education - just develop the habit of including them in the process of working things out.

WEIGHTS AND MEASURES

Despite government efforts to make Britain conform to European standards, Imperial measures (miles, feet, inches, pounds, onces etc.) remain in common usage in everyday life, whilst schools teach Metric measurements (kilometres, metres, kilograms, grams etc.)

In order to avoid causing your child confusion it is therefore advisable to teach both Imperial and Metric neasurements, but then to concentrate mainly upon the Metric.

  Many recipes still use pounds and ounces, so when cooking you will often use Imperial measure.

When working out problems, Metric measurements are much, much easier to deal with than Imperial measurements.

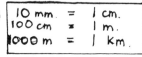

10 mm	=	1 cm.
100 cm	=	1 m.
1000 m	=	1 km.

Britain still uses miles per hour on the roads, but goods can now be bought just as readily by the metre as by the yard.

As well as being easy to work with, Metric measurements also provide valuable practice in working with decimals. They also lend themselves to being used with a calculator, which Imperial measurements do not.

DECIMALS

Once a child can work out problems to do with money, weights and measurements, then they will have a good working understanding of decimals.

Teachers are often surprised that children do not understand the theory of decimals but in fact, decimals are quite an advanced mathematical concept, and it was only a few hundred years ago that they were introduced to Western civilisation.

hundreds tens units • tenths hundredths thousandths

$$394.735$$

If your child can add, subtract, multiply and divide by decimals, then they will have gained a good grounding in the study both of Arithmetic and of Mathematics.

FURTHER STUDY

Arithmetic is similar to reading in that a child will have bursts of interest interspersed with periods of not wanting to do sums. The Home Educating parent does not have to hold back a child who becomes really interested in numbers, and does not have to push a child who is not yet ready to absorb a particular aspect of them.

Once you have established a good grounding in Arithmetic (maybe by the age of 11 or 12), you can either go on to study Mathematics or else leave it and allow your child to take the initiative for further study at a later date.

A few people study Mathematics because they enjoy it; most people study it because they need a GCSE. An intelligent young person with a good understanding of Arithmetic is quite capable of following a one year course to get a good GCSE pass in Mathematics. The course could be from books, by Correspondence, at Evening Class, at College or by private tuition.

CREATIVE PLAY

Whilst it is important that a young child should learn to read, write and do Arithmetic, they will actually be learning more through their play.

This is particularly true up to the age of seven, but children up to the age of eleven, twelve and beyond still need to play.

The nature of a child's play is largely determined by where they live, the company that they keep and the sort of toys that they have.

A parent who wishes their child to play constructively has to provide a rich and varied environment. Unfortunately, many of the facilities and activities provided for children in our society tend to stifle their imagination and are lacking in aesthetic beauty.

A very important aspect of Home Education is to make your home as interesting a place as possible for children to play.

TELEVISION

Television is definitely not an asset in terms of play. Watching television stimulates the mind without giving any opportunity for participation. A child cannot join in with the programme that is being watched, cannot talk to the characters, cannot touch them and cannot change the course of the plot. The child sits and absorbs what is being shown, and has no control over what is happening. This is the exact opposite of constructive play.

To make matters worse, television programme makers have developed a particular style to attract a child's attention. This frequently involves rapid scene changes, garish colours and in cartoons, ritualised violence. Advertisements follow the same pattern, repeatedly appealing to a child's desire for a particular object, and making it appear more attractive than it really is.

Watching television overstimulates the mind

whilst not involving the body, leaving a child confused and restless.

For this reason, television cannot be counted as being educational for young children, and should be avoided as much as possible.

For many children, television has the power of an hypnotic drug, and if it is in the room they cannot help switching it on and sinking into a dazed stupor while they watch. It is therefore often a good idea not to have a television in the room most commonly used by the children. If you have a television it can be discreetly placed elsewhere in the house.

MODERN TOYS

Many modern toys derive their appeal solely from their connection with television. They either represent characters seen on television, or else are heavily advertised.

Most parents have cupboards full of such toys (many of them broken) that have provided very little play value and were discarded after the initial burst of interest.

There are a few notable exceptions to this general trend (usually the more expensive ones, unfortunately), such as Lego, some train sets and a wide variety of dolls and soft toys, and these are obviously worth collecting when finances allow.

Most modern toys are made of plastic – it is easy to mass produce, relatively cheap and usually safe. There is no reason to suppose that there is anything wrong with plastic, but children benefit from being able to play with as wide a variety of materials and substances as possible, and ideally a range of non-plastic toys should also be provided.

TRADITIONAL TOYS
WOODEN BLOCKS

A collection of wooden blocks of different shapes and sizes, some painted and others not, can give endless hours of play to a young child, as

they experiment with arranging the bricks in any of the infinite possible permutations. Such a collection can be added to as new pieces of wood come your way.

DOLLS

Good quality, hand-made dolls always hold a special place in the heart of a child.

Such dolls are difficult to come across and can be expensive, but it is possible to make them yourself. (see book list)

WOODEN ANIMALS

Most children love animals and like to incorporate them in their play.

Wooden animals are usually more durable and easier to hold than their plastic equivalents.

JIG-SAW PUZZLES

These provide hours of fascination for most children.

DRESSING-UP CLOTHES

A collection of old clothes, hats, gloves, shoes etc. combined with any costumes (nurse, policeman etc.) that you have, provides an enormous amount of fun and entertainment. It doesn't matter if half the clothes are too big. These can be supplemented with old sheets or pieces of material that can be used to drape over things, to make houses, as well as being worn to make outlandish costumes.

PLAY HOUSE

Children do have vivid imaginations and do not have to be provided with an elaborate structure in order to play houses.

Clothes horses draped in cloths, a bedside cabinet for a cooker, and some small saucepans from the kitchen provide a child with the necessary ingredients.

Dolls' tea sets and little cutlery add to the fun enormously.

GENERAL

In addition to toys, try to make available lots of paper, different types of crayons, different types of modelling material and access to the open air. These all offer interesting possibilities to a child. Of course, this list is not comprehensive, but it should convey the idea that it is relatively easy to make a home into a place where a child feels that they have an unlimited number of things to do and need never feel bored.

YOUNG CHILDREN - OTHER SUBJECTS

The preceding pages outline the essential ingredients of Primary Education - Reading, Writing, Arithmetic and Playing. Being at home with your child, however, gives you the opportunity of involving them in a wide range of other activities.

These activities are not only interesting and useful in their own right but also lay the foundation for study at Secondary level of Education, and for work in the outside world.

GARDENING

All life on this planet depends upon plants being able to capture the Sun's energy They use it for growth and, in the process, purify the air.

All animals, both carnivorous and vegetarian, are ultimately dependent on the plentiful supply of plants.

This is such an important fact that it should be learnt through practical experience, not as a thing taught in a classroom.

Children who learn at home can plant seeds, watch them grow, transplant them into the garden, water them, protect them from pests, weed round them and eventually reap the harvest of food or flowers.

This experience is impossible to recreate

in school, as plants die during the holidays. At the height of the summer, in August, all schools are closed, and there is noone to tend them.

Although it is an advantage to have a large garden, a child can learn just as much by tending window boxes and hanging baskets, if you live in a flat or house with no garden.

FLOWERS AND VEGETABLES

All children have a great interest in food, and the experience of actually watching food grow (not just the traditional mustard and cress) fills them with excitement and anticipation.

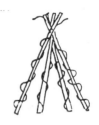

Flowers also hold a special place in a child's life, and being able to grow them themselves gives children a sense of pride and achievement.

THE SEASONS

Gardening is by far the best way of introducing a child to the changes that take place in the course of a year. They learn to see the world through the eyes of their plants as well as through their own experiences.

THE ENVIRONMENT

It is hard to believe that the world would be in the state that it is today if all the industrialists, scientists and exploiters of the environment had grown up with a love of Nature. Gardening is the perfect introduction to the Biological Sciences and a study of the Environment.

115

MUSIC

Music does not fit well into a school timetable. Individual tuition means that children miss other lessons, and it is impossible to allow thirty children in a class to practise at the same time - except on the simplest instruments.

The situation at home could not be more different. The child's instrument is always at hand, and they can practise whenever the mood takes them.

THE RECORDER

It is common to teach children to play the recorder from the age of about six or seven.

The instrument is cheap, easy to play and suitable for small fingers. If you cannot play it yourself already, you will find that you can soon pick it up with the aid of a simple instruction manual.

With the help of a recorder a child can learn to read music, to play beautiful tunes and to experiment with music. (See Book List)

MUSIC LESSONS

If a child enjoys playing the recorder or any other instruments that you have in the house, then they will probably want to play another instrument when they are a little older.

The piano and the guitar are popular choices but children are drawn to a wide range of instruments.

Unless you play the instrument yourself you

will have to find a music teacher. Sometimes the availability of a tutor dictates the instrument. The Home Educated child is fortunate in that they can select a time for their lesson that is convenient for them and their teacher. It does not have to be squeezed in at the end of a long and tiring school day.

In the same way, practice does not have to be restricted to spare moments in the evenings, but can be done at any time of the day when there are not more pressing things to be done.

LEARNING TOGETHER

If you never learnt to play an instrument when you were young, or else you were forced to learn against your will and have since forgotten everything that you were taught, then now is your chance to learn to play.

It is enormous fun going over tunes with your children as they learn them, and it is usually much easier for an adult than it is for a child, so you should not find their pace too taxing.

As in many other areas, Home Education can be as much for yourself as for your child.

MUSICAL APPRECIATION

Whatever your own taste in music, it is very enjoyable to listen to recordings of great works of music with your children. Neither of you need make any pretence of great expertise, and can just discuss whether you enjoyed listening to it or not.

Most big libraries have extensive collections of records, tapes and C.D.'s that you can borrow for a small charge, so this need not be a very expensive exercise.

You can also introduce children to your own musical favourites, and let them know in what way you find them to be moving.

HOUSEWORK

Unfortunately the work involved in running and maintaining a home is not valued in the way that it should be in our society. As a result, schools are embarassed about teaching housework and give it names that they think make it more acceptable, such as "Home Economics".

In fact, young children love housework and are desp rate to help their mothers and fathers with work around the house. If you let them join in when they are little, do not isolate them from home by sending them to school as they grow older, and give them more responsibility as and when they can cope with it, then they will develop into young people who automatically play their full part in the life of the home.

COOKING

Cooking is almost like magic for young children. Nothing gives them more pleasure than mixing ingredients together and making them into biscuits, bread and cakes.

Letting them help with the cooking can slow you down, but it is worth it for the pleasure that it gives them. The more cooking that you let them do, the more aware they will become of what they are and are not capable of doing, and also of how much work goes into preparing meals.

It is not long before they become capable of preparing small meals, such as breakfast and lunch, themselves.

WASHING UP

It is surprising to adults that children get almost as much pleasure from washing up as they do from cooking. They love playing with water and soap.

Being little, they do have a tendency to make a mess, but are quite capable of understanding that if they create puddles in the kitchen then they will not be allowed to wash up again.

You have to be the judge of when to take over if you think that they are getting tired or if there is too much for them to do.

CLEANING

Dusting, hoovering and polishing are all activities that children enjoy - especially if you are doing them at the same time.

Tidying away toys can cause problems, but most children can understand a simple idea such as having to put away the toys that they are playing with before getting any more out.

OBJECTIVES

Noone really minds being a slave to the needs of a baby but similarly, noone wants to have to tend to the every need of a sixteen year old.

By involving your children in work around the house from a very young age, you allow them gradually to take more and more responsibility for themselves.

Not only is this a relief to you, but it is also invaluable to them, as it gives them the ideal preparation for one day setting up their own home.

WOODWORK

You will probably never be able to mimic the facilities of a well-stocked school workshop in your home, but you will be able to offer your child the far more worthwhile opportunity of building up, and working with, a tool kit of their own.

YOUNG CHILDREN

Up until the age of about ten or eleven, children cannot really be entrusted with wood-working tools, as the risk of cuts and bruises is too great.

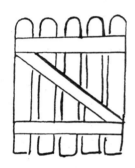

They can, however, help you in jobs that you are doing by banging in nails, helping to saw and especially by sanding down bits of wood.

If they are involved in jobs, such as making a garden gate, a hutch for their animals or a shelf in the house, then the idea of the value of being able to make things in wood takes a firm hold in their minds.

OLDER CHILDREN

Older children can work with saws and chisels, and can start to devise their own projects. If you are not particularly skilled at woodwork yourself there are many books available which describe carving, whittling, making joints and other techniques of wood-work.

Although a child can use your tools, you should let them start to make their own collection.

Learning to care for their tools is an essential part of learning to work with wood.

HANDCRAFTS

If you love crafts yourself then you will not need any encouragement to introduce them to your children, and will probably know the best way to go about it.

If you were never taught crafts properly yourself and have had no opportunity to learn since then, the following suggestions may act as a useful guide as to how to begin.

WEAVING ON A CARD

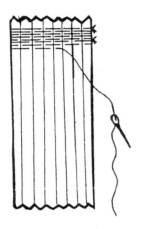

Children as young as five can do this.

Cut notches in either end of a piece of very thick card and wrap the "warp" thread between the notches. Heavy dishcloth cotton is good for this.

Then weave your wool with the aid of an embroidery needle, going round and round from the front to the back of the card. Join threads at one side. This makes a tube which can be continued further on the back than on the front, to make a flap. To finish off you cut the warp threads and knot them together. The purse is slipped off the card, turned inside out and lined with a contrasting scrap of material. This ensures that the ends are out of sight, and gives strength to the finished product.

Very attractive purses and pencil cases can be made in this way.

EMBROIDERY

This can also be started with children as

young as five years.

They can learn to do a variety of stitches whilst making bookmarks, place mats and serviette rings on binca – a material that can be purchased from Craft shops. $\frac{1}{4}$ metre will give several bookmarks.

Embroidery is a relaxing and rewarding pastime. Once they have learnt the basic stitches, children can continue to develop their skills and make ever more intricate designs for years to come. Making a backing for an embroidered item teaches the skills which will later be useful in sewing.

KNITTING

The invention of modern machines has led to knitted garments being available in the shops at prices cheaper than one has to pay for the wool from which they are made.

Knitting is, therefore, not such an important part of everyday life as it was fifty years ago, when it was common for people to knit their own gloves, socks, jumpers etc.

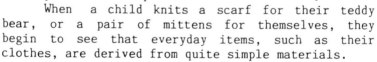

People who knit nowadays usually do so for pleasure, or to create a special garment not available in the shops.

This does not diminish the value of teaching a child to knit. The modern world is a very intimidating place for a child because it is full of so many things that are beyond their comprehension.

When a child knits a scarf for their teddy bear, or a pair of mittens for themselves, they begin to see that everyday items, such as their clothes, are derived from quite simple materials.

Knitting itself is very easy (it is just patterns that may be difficult to follow), and a

122

series of worksheets is available giving advice on how to introduce knitting to a child (see Book List).

CROCHET

If you start to become interested in crafts, you will probably want to have a go at crochet. In some ways it is easier than knitting, as you only have one hook, instead of two needles, and there is not the same hazard of dropped stitches.

SEWING

Young children find a needle and thread too small to work with, with ease. Sewing is best introduced to children when they are a little older — maybe in their early teens.

ART

As a home educator you have the advantage of being able to ensure that any Art materials that you buy are properly looked after and are not wasted or destroyed by thoughtless or stupid behaviour.

You can therefore afford to build up a good collection so that you can experiment with a range of different materials.

If you are good at Art, you can pass on your knowledge to your child. If you aren't then, as in many other areas of Home Education, you have the opportunity to learn with your child. You will probably find that much of your problem is not due to a lack of ability, but rather to a lack of encouragement when you were young.

DRAWING

Young children produce more pleasing results with thick wax crayons which they can hold easily and with which they can fill the page in bold colours.

Older children appreciate a really good set of coloured pencils, with which they can do detailed pictures.

You can also use oil pastels or charcoal if you want to experiment and, when they get older, your child may like to try pencil drawing.

PAINTING

Liquid paints are, in many ways, better than the block paints often sold in toy shops. When you are painting make sure that you are well organised with lots of paper (thick lining paper is quite good), and lots of clean water to hand. Don't try working with too many different colours at one go, and only mix up small quantities so that you don't have too much waste.

As your child gets older, try getting ideas from Art books and making copies of pictures that you like. This helps them to improve their technique. You can also visit Art Galleries (which are usually free) to see the originals of acclaimed works of Art.

MODELLING

Modelling is a very valuable exercise. Making models of animals and people is particularly good experience, and models can be made to illustrate work done in other subjects such as History or Geography.

PLASTICINE, BEESWAX, PLAY DOUGH ETC.
There are many different types of modelling materials available, each one has different properties and you have to experiment with them to discover what kind of models they will produce.

While children will make models on their own, they usually prefer you to join in and help them with ideas. These models can be kept for a short while and then the material can be reused.

BREAD DOUGH, MARZIPAN ETC.
These are edible materials, often with similar modelling properties as the above, and children obviously get extra pleasure from using them. If you make bread it is a good idea to give a child some dough to make shapes, which you then bake.

CLAY
Few people have a kiln in their home so you will probably be unable to fire any clay models that you make. Clay is still probably the best

modelling material. You can make models and then break them up when you have finished (make sure that you keep the clay moist), or you can buy clay which is mixed with nylon filaments, which is quite strong when it dries, and can be painted and varnished to make very attractive models.

OTHER MATERIALS

Craft shops sell modelling materials that set hard to make permanent models, but these are often quite expensive.

Plaster of Paris can be used to make models - normally with the aid of a mould, and quite intricate models can be made of Papier Mache. The more time that you spend making models then the more ideas you will have.

GAMES

PLAYING CARDS, DRAUGHTS, CHESS, BOARD GAMES ETC.

There can be no doubt that these sorts of games are educational, enjoyable, develop the mind and confer social skills useful in later life.

Playing cards, in particular, provide a wide range of games which, on the one hand, help a young child to recognise numbers whilst, on the other hand, teach an older child to weigh up complex probabilities of success depending upon various distributions of cards. (In fact, many of the great advances in Mathematics made during the Renaissance were made by men who spent much of their time at the gaming tables.)

Draughts and chess obviously develop powers of reasoning and planning. Lexicon and Scrabble are excellent for developing vocabulary and grammar.

EDUCATIONAL GAMES

In addition to conventional games there are many games specifically designed to teach certain skills such as Reading or Arithmetic. These games can be particularly useful for children with reading difficulties, or whose experience of school has made them unable to face written work.

Other games test General Knowledge or concentrate on a particular subject such as History.

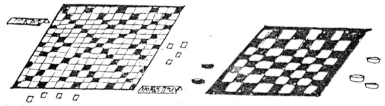

Time spent playing games with your children is not time wasted. As well as being enjoyable, playing games makes a valuable contribution to their education.

SPORT AND PHYSICAL EDUCATION

Sport and P.E. lessons are essential in school, where so much of the time is spent sitting behind desks.

You have to judge how much exercise your children are getting in the routine that you have devised, and how much it needs to be supplemented with sporting activities.

SWIMMING

You can ask your local baths what time of the week they are most quiet - usually a weekday when no schools attend - and get in the habit of going for a relaxing swim on that day.

TENNIS, BADMINTON ETC.

The same is true of Tennis and Badminton. There are usually times in the week when courts are hardly used at all, and you can enjoy a long session without worrying about making a fool of yourself or holding other people up.

HORSE RIDING, ICE SKATING

Depending upon your finances and local facilities, these activities can also be a source of pleasure and exercise.

TEAM GAMES

If you are friendly with other Home Educators then trips to the swimming baths or tennis courts are often a good time to meet up.

If you have a child who desperately wants to be part of a football team, then they will have to join a local club. These often offer a higher standard of coaching than school teams, as many schools no longer play Saturday fixtures and restrict their sport activities to normal school hours.

LANGUAGES

If you can speak a second language quite well, you should have no problem in teaching a young child, and you can then continue learning together.

If, like the majority of British people, you can speak no language but English, then you should consider starting to learn another.

WALES

Traditionally, English people have not rated the importance of learning modern languages very highly, but vociferous campaigns from Welsh speakers have led to Welsh speaking schools being established in Wales. These schools ensure that their pupils are bilingual and have become just as popular with English speaking families as with Welsh speakers. This is because they achieve much better examination results which is, at least partly, due to the fact that becoming fluent in a second language develops the mind and makes it better able to tackle other problems.

CHOOSING A LANGUAGE

Some languages are more useful than others. You should choose one with which you have some familiarity, which you are confident of being able to learn and which your child will have some opportunity to speak.

French and German are prominent languages in the European Community, Spanish may be useful on holiday, is the language of South America and is commonly spoken in the U.S.A., and Russian is widely spoken in the former Soviet block countries.

You could choose to study any of these languages, or alternatively may have some personal or family connection with a part of the world where another language is spoken.

It is very difficult to learn a language from a book, but you can buy tapes or borrow them from the Library; follow Television and Radio courses;

go to Evening Classes or pay for private lessons. Using a combination should enable you to pick up enough of the basis of a language to start teaching your child.

TEACHING A LANGUAGE

This is not as difficult as you might expect. The teaching of Modern Languages is the subject most difficult to adapt to the classroom because each child has so few opportunities to speak it on their own.

When you are teaching your own child they can repeat words and phrases as you teach them, and have a go at making up sentences.

A workbook of songs, games and phrases useful in the teaching of French is available (see Book List).

Once you achieve a certain standard you can follow television courses etc. with your child, and practise with each other. It doesn't matter if you make mistakes. Children learning their first language construct some quite odd sentences, but eventually learn to adapt to the common usage -- you will do the same with your second or third languages.

TRAVEL ABROAD

Being with native speakers of a language is the only way of becoming really fluent.

As a Home Educator you may be limited by finances but you will not be limited by your child having to attend school, and you may find it is possible to live abroad for a while. If so, this is the perfect way to learn a foreign language.

Alternatively you may be able to afford an extended holiday abroad -- travel is much cheaper when you are not restricted to school holiday dates.

Exchange visits with European teenagers are no problem to arrange, as English is the language that most people on the Continent feel is essential for their children to learn.

TEACHING OLDER CHILDREN

Most of the subjects already discussed continue to be relevant when the child reaches the age of Secondary Education, and obviously you should not have to make a sudden change in your routine when your child reaches their eleventh birthday!

However, as the child develops into a young adult, some subjects gain a new importance, special interests are developed and he or she starts to take more responsibility for their work.

Some people show a definite inclination towards academic work, others have practical interests, while most retain an interest in all activities that they have been doing.

Home Education does not lose its appeal at this stage or become unable to meet the demands of a teenager. On the contrary, it gives a young person the freedom that they need. It is the absence of this freedom that causes so many of the problems and frustrations of our Secondary Schools.

Young people between the ages of eleven and sixteen undergo a lot of changes, and have to start to take their place in Society as adults. They have to come to terms with all the pressing social issues of our time such as sex, drugs and crime, as well as preparing themselves for employment and work.

Unfortunately, the Education system has forced Secondary Schools to concentrate most of their efforts upon work for GCSE examinations. Important aspects of a child's education and development are therefore often neglected.

The Home Educated child does not need to suffer in this way, but you will need to have a good understanding of the GCSE system in order to have the confidence to continue with Home Education. For this reason, the next few pages are devoted to discussing how GCSEs relate to the Home Educated child.

GCSEs - NOT DOING THEM

If you and your child decide not to do GCSEs, it does not mean that you are choosing a second rate education. Much of the work done for GCSEs is not in itself useful or interesting, and you may be able to fill your time much more constructively when freed from its restraints.

Employers always complain about the sort of work done by children in school, and say that it does not prepare them for real jobs. They will always be prepared to listen to a young person who has not been to school and has something different to offer.

Once a young person has had one job then it is their work experience that will count with a new employer, and not the number of GCSEs that they have.

Society is much less rigid than it used to be, and a young person can choose to go to College or Evening Classes and sit GCSEs at any time that they like. Alternatively, once they are twenty one, they can enter Higher Education as mature students (without qualifications), and can go on to professional careers if they wish.

Not doing GCSEs at sixteen does not limit choice, and does not condemn a young person to a life of second class employment.

GCSEs - DOING THEM

WHO NEEDS GCSEs?
Maths and English GCSEs are useful to any young person looking for a job.

The main reason for sitting other GCSEs is to gain entry to 'A' level courses and to Higher Education. They are not, however, always essential - articulate and well motivated young people are able to gain a place on some Further Education courses without having any recognised qualifications.

GCSEs are not of much direct relevance to young people who decide to leave the education system at the age of sixteen and start to make their own way in the world.

Some young people, however, view GCSEs as an interesting challenge, giving them a standard against which to measure their achievement even if they do not intend to go on to do 'A' levels.

PREPARATION FOR GCSEs
Despite statements to the contrary, the entire Secondary School curriculum and timetable is geared towards getting GCSE passes. Even so the actual syllabus, and any course work required, is covered in the two years leading up to the exam.

A young person studying at home for a GCSE in a subject in which they are interested, needs only one year to cover the syllabus, and a fifteen year old can easily tackle five GCSEs in a year.

There is therefore no pressure to make decisions when your child is eleven. You can wait, and if your child decides that they want to go in for a career that requires 'A' levels, then they can make their decision when they are fifteen.

This leaves you time to continue following a broad-based curriculum for a few more years, which should result in your child being more mature and having more to say when they do do their GCSEs.

BOOKS

By the time that they are fifteen, your child should be skilled at working from books, and should have no trouble working through course books and revision guides for GCSEs. You should not find this work very difficult yourself if you have been working with your child up to this point, and will therefore be able to help.

PAST PAPERS

Past papers, obtainable from the Examination Board, are an obvious source of extra study material. (see address list.)

CORRESPONDENCE COURSES/PRIVATE TUITION/EVENING CLASSES

If you are particularly worried about one or two subjects, then you can invest in a Correspondence course or private tuition, to ensure that your child gets the help that they need.

Alternatively, they can enrol in an Evening Class in these subjects - this may be particularly useful if they wish to learn something that requires specialist equipment which you don't possess - such as a word processor.

COLLEGE COURSES

If your child doesn't mind waiting until they are sixteen they can go to College, either full-time or part-time, and do five or more GCSEs - and possibly an 'A' level at the same time to make the work more interesting.

In this case they would be mainly working with people of their own age who have chosen to do "re-sits".

ENTERING THE EXAM

If your child has chosen to study at Evening Class or College, then they will be entered for the exam automatically (and will not have to pay).

If they are studying at home then you will have to arrange for them to sit the exam at a local examination centre. Adult Education Centres (Evening Classes) are usually the most helpful, but

Schools and Colleges should also take external candidates. If you have any problems, then your regional Examining Board will help you. They will also arrange a Moderator to assess any coursework involved in the GCSE that your child is doing.
(see address list)

GOING TO SCHOOL

Home educated children can choose to go to school - with their parents' consent - and may decide that this is the best way to get their GCSEs. In that case, the best time to join is the beginning of year ten (fourth year), as then they are present for the whole syllabus. If they join in year eleven (when they are fifteen), they will have to work hard to catch up with areas of the syllabus that have already been covered.

Schools are relatively civilised at this stage. An uneasy truce usually exists between pupils and staff, and classes have sorted themselves out into those which are going to work for exams and those which are going to do nothing. Home educated children who enter such a situation normally quite enjoy themselves.

MONEY AND WORK

One of the biggest causes of concern to children is their lack of access to money. Without money they cannot buy anything. As they get older, this concern becomes a deeper sense of frustration and annoyance.

Teenagers need to buy clothes, records, tapes, C.D.s etc.; they need money for transport and holidays and money for going out in the evening. Their only legitimate sources of money are gifts from their parents, and poorly paid casual work that can be fitted in outside school hours.

Neither of these options is satisfactory and it is not surprising that many teenagers feel bitter about the way in which they are deprived of money, and that some turn to petty crime.

WHEN IS THE BEST TIME TO START EARNING MONEY?

It is easy to see how present conditions have arisen - children were terribly exploited in the eighteenth and nineteenth centuries, being made to do dangerous and unpleasant work for very little money.

Eventually legislation was brought in to outlaw the use of child labour, and we now have laws that prevent people under the age of sixteen from being employed in anything but on a part-time basis.

Young people, however, are still entitled to earn money using their own initiative, and when you teach your child at home you can develop some of your activities into ways of enabling your child to earn money. This may be started from a young age and allowed to build up as they become aware of a greater need for money. Ideally they can learn to balance their income and expenditure, and to work harder when they need more money.

WHAT SHOULD CHILDREN BE PAID FOR?

Some parents develop a system of paying their children for doing jobs around the home such as washing the car, cleaning the windows, tidying their rooms etc.

This can be counterproductive as children may then refuse to do the housework for which they are not paid.

It is much better to initiate activities that bring fresh income into the home. However, many jobs that young people do, such as delivering papers or washing cars, provide few long-term benefits and, if possible, you should encourage projects that involve creativity and imagination such as:-

CRAFT STALLS

You can sell your and your child's handwork at Craft Fairs. Christmas is the best time for this and in addition to the items already discussed, you can make jewellery, Christmas Cards and decorations.

PLANTS

You can sell seedlings and young plants, that you grow in the garden, at Summer fairs, car boot sales and Sunday markets that are held throughout the Summer.

PRODUCE

If you have a large fruit and vegetable garden you may be able to find an outlet for surplus produce with your child doing much of the picking and packing and keeping a fair share of the takings.

BAKING

You may be able to sell cakes and biscuits that you bake, for a profit.

Obviously, these are only examples and, depending on the type of work that you do and the age of your child, there are countless ways in which you can earn money. A young person does not have to pay housing and basic living costs; they do not, therefore, need a large income.

It is much better to give them the means of earning a few pounds per week than having constant arguments about the levels of pocket money.

TRAINING FOR WORK

This type of activity can be not only remunerative and enjoyable, but it can be a useful training for work in adult life.

- it provides experience in running a small business

- it teaches a young person just how much work is required to make money

- it could lead directly into a means of making a living - either by expanding your activity into a business or by encouraging a young person to get a job in a similar field

- It can provide a real incentive to go in for Higher Education if a young person becomes aware that they require particular skills to pursue the matter further.

WHAT IS THE LEGALITY OF THIS TYPE OF WORK!

It is your duty to ensure that your child receives full time education but, as has been discussed in a previous chapter, it is difficult to define what this means in terms of hours spent in formal lessons.

Two hours per day of one -to -one tuition during term-time would probable qualify. Much of the education that takes place in the home does not stop during school holidays or weekends - the education that you provide is not separate from the rest of the child's life.

Home educated children are usually, therefore, receiving an amount of education far in excess of the amount necessary to meet the "full-time" requirement. If they choose to spend part of their days in activities that lead to them earning some money, then this still does not mean that they are not in receipt of "full-time" education.

SEX EDUCATION

From a biological point of view, the prime aim of any living thing is to reproduce, and every other need is subservient to that. It is not surprising, therefore, that human beings experience intense sexual feelings, particularly when they first reach sexual maturity.

One of the most important duties of education is to prepare young people for this experience and to help them adapt their feelings and desires to the social conditions of the times.

Unfortunately, the schools are unable to meet this need, and their failure to do so is potentially very dangerous for the children who attend.

SEX AND SCHOOLS

The problem originates from the time that a child first starts going to school. Children are made to feel that adults represent a remote authority and that classmates are their only allies.

As years pass, the child learns never to open up to, or express their feelings to, their teachers, while teachers find themselves having to restrict the freedom of the children in their care. In order to maintain order, teachers have to limit simple activities such as talking and walking around the classroom. They have to enforce rules which prohibit chewing gum and smoking, and also give lectures about the evils of drinking and drug taking, adult videos, joy riding etc.

By the time that a child reaches adolescence teachers, and by extension all adults, have come to represent an irrational, dictatorial authority that tries to prevent children from enjoying all the things that are considered enjoyable in our society.

When teachers start to talk about the dangers of promiscuity, under age sex, unwanted pregnancies, AIDS and Venereal Disease they have little chance of being listened to with an open mind. As far as young people are concerned it is simply another case of adults trying to spoil their fun. They ignore the advice and experiment in secret - as they do with everything else that they are told not to do - often with disastrous results.

This state of affairs can be easily avoided for the Home Educated child.

SEX EDUCATION AND YOUNG CHILDREN

Nothing is more natural than for young children to ask their parents where they have come from. When they are very young they do not usually understand detailed biological explanations, and are content to know only the essential facts.

When they go to school, children often stop talking to their parents about where babies come from. At school, much of the talk between children involves innuendo, smutty jokes and half truths about sex, and children quickly pick up the idea that it is a subject not to be talked about in front of adults.

This does not happen to children taught at home, and the subject of where they have come from need never become taboo.

NATURE STUDY

You will find that conversations about reproduction will arise when you are working in the garden, looking after your pets, walking in the countryside, watching birds and when you are studying the life cycles of living things.

By working with, and talking about, nature you are allowing your child to appreciate the overwhelming drive that living things have to reproduce.

FAMILY LIFE

By choosing to teach your child at home, you will be a living example to your child of the work required in bringing up a human being. Children taught at home value beyond measure the fact that their parents have chosen to look after them at home rather than send them off to be looked after by someone else at school.

You can expect that they will automatically give the same amount of time to their own children, and will have no illusions that being a parent is an easy duty that can lightly be passed on to someone else.

TEACHING THE "FACTS OF LIFE" TO YOUR CHILDREN

Parents often feel embarassed to talk about the facts of life with their children when the latter start to reach sexual maturity.

The problems are heightened if they themselves never discussed sex with their parents, and if the subject has not been mentioned in the home from the time that the child started going to school at the age of 5.

These problems do not exist for home educating families because

– the child is able to continue asking simple questions and receiving simple answers throughout their childhood.

– by studying plants and animals with their parents, a child is able to make comparisons between human reproduction and that which they see in nature.

– the wider social life available to a home educated child means that they are more likely to spend time with babies and young children.

The main points that you hope that your child will pick up from this education are

– the link between sex and babies

– the number of years of care and love that a human baby needs before it reaches maturity

– the benefit to the child (and the mother and father) if the child is conceived in a loving permanent relationship.

If your child is aware of these fundamental points, then they will be able to discuss the various moral and health issues connected to sex on a firm basis of understanding.

141

The issues that young people want to discuss are:

MARRIAGE – is marriage a worthwhile institution or should they just live with someone that they love?

LOVE – what is the love that exists between two people? What does it feel like? How do you recognise it? Does it last?

SEX BEFORE MARRIAGE – If they intend to marry someone should they have sex beforehand? If so, when? If they intend never to marry, at what stage of a relationship is sex appropriate?

HOMOSEXUALITY – what does it mean? What does it feel like to be Gay?

CONTRACEPTION – Is contraception right? Is abstinence better? What are the facts about different types of contraception? Do they work?

PROTECTION – Is there such a thing as safe sex? If so, what is it?

AIDS – What is it? Is it always lethal? Who catches it? What should they do about it? What is the difference between HIV and AIDS?

It may be a mistake for you to try and give answers to these questions. They are personal and everyone has to reach their own solutions. However, you are more experienced than your child and, out of everyone, your views are the ones that they will most respect. After all, their life has arisen from your answers to these questions.

Therefore, by creating a lifestyle for your family in which these issues can be discussed, you are doing your children a real service, and are fulfilling your ultimate duty as a parent.

142

ACADEMIC STUDIES

In theory, the main purpose of Secondary Schools is to cater for children who have academic leanings.

In modern conditions, however, even these children can be served better at home, for the following reasons:

- Modern schools tend to be at either end of two extremes. They are either underresourced and demoralised, and not able to offer a very good education or else their obsession with GCSE results precludes all other work (both academic and nonacademic), and pupils therefore receive a very stilted education.
- Social aspects of schools can lead children into dangerous areas such as drugs, drinking, sex etc.
- Society itself is now so threatening to young people that they benefit from a more positive inclusion in the family until a later age.
- The huge amount of knowledge now available makes the school syllabuses seem limited and unimaginative.
- Many learning techniques and teaching aids are more suited to home use than school use.
- Home taught children have more control over their studies and can therefore make better use of their time, cover a lot more work, study more subjects and retain a much greater interest in what they are doing.

NON-ACADEMIC PUPILS

Although our educational system labels at least 60% of people as being educational failures, there is no reason for any Home Educated child to feel in any way inadequate.

A child whose family is not academic and who themselves develops a great interest in practical subjects can still follow all the subjects discussed in the next few pages. They do not have to keep written records of their work and do not have to sit GCSEs, but this doesn't mean that they do not enjoy and understand what they have done.

All young people being educated at home should therefore at least consider including some work in the following subjects in their weekly routine.

ENGLISH

READING

One of the best ways of giving young children an interest in books, and therefore a desire to read, is to read to them every night before they go to bed.

There is no reason ever to stop this practice. The older your child is then the more interesting the books become to you, as well as to them.

Once you start a book you don't have to stop for holidays or weekends or if your child is ill, you just keep on going. Books that you might not feel inclined to read yourself become gripping when read at the rate of one or two chapters per night.

In this way you can read several classics of English literature per year. You don't have to discuss and analyse the books, it is quite obvious what you enjoy and what you do not.

If you are reading books together then your child will almost certainly want to read other books on their own.

If your child has reading difficulties, then reading to them in this way will result in them having a much better knowledge of English literature than their contemporaries who can read with ease.

WRITING

By introducing your child to the great works of English literature, you will be giving them the background knowledge which will allow them to write well.

Spelling, grammar, punctuation and vocabulary are all improved by reading good quality writing.

144

To a certain extent, your child's own inclination will determine how much writing they do. Some children are very drawn to creative writing and will write stories from a young age, and may then progress onto writing novels when they are in their teens. Others show little interest in writing and it would be wrong to force them.

POETRY

You will also get much pleasure from reading poetry with your child.

You can select favourite poems to learn by heart. At home this is not the onerous task that it can be at school, but rather it is a source of much enjoyment and pleasure.

Children with reading difficulties can make tapes of their favourite poems and learn from these.

You can also make up books of the child's favourite poetry or of poetry that they write themselves and illustrate them with your child's drawings.

DRAMA

Young people wishing to take part in plays can join local theatre groups, especially Youth Theatres. Younger children can produce their own plays, with your help. The fact that they are only produced for a few friends and relatives does not detract from the enjoyment of all concerned.

You can read your favourite plays with your child, and can read a play through before it is to appear at your nearest theatre, and then go and see it.

In this way your child can become familiar with Shakespeare plays without any of the difficulties that arise at school.

MATHEMATICS

Mathematics is one of the most elegant and intrinsically satisfying areas of study available to a young person. The laws of Mathematics appear to owe their existence to a power incomprehensible to the human mind, and in trying to master this subject one comes face to face with the most fundamental questions of life.

The science of Mathematics has been developed by philosophers and, in the past, Mathematics and Philosophy were inextricably linked. It is therefore a travesty that this most noble of sciences has been reduced to being the subject of derision and hatred amongst school children.

There is no reason to impose a study of Mathematics upon everyone, Very few people require a knowledge of Mathematics in order to pursue their careers. Most people would be far better off if their education restricted itself to a thorough grounding in the use of Arithmetic. People would then be free to pursue the study of Mathematics as, and when, the inclination took them.

This should be the case with Home Educated children.

Areas worthy of interest include ALGEBRA, GEOMETRY, MODERN MATHS, CALCULUS and NUMBER THEORY. GCSE textbooks tend not to present this work in a very interesting fashion, but there are a whole range of Maths books available in most bookshops.

If your child is not very interested in Mathematics but needs a Maths GCSE to go on to Further Education, then you must ensure that they have a good understanding of Arithmetic.

They will then be able to undertake a one year study course in Mathematics (from books, at Evening classes or by Correspondence course) when they are fifteen, and should pass their GCSE with ease. Children are put off Mathematics when made to study it year after year when they have no interest in it, and cannot understand what is being talked about.

146

SCIENCE

The idea of Science teaching fills a lot of parents with concern. In practice, the fact that Home Education is fully integrated and that different subjects are not rigidly separated means that Science is well covered by Home Educating families.

The purpose of Science is to discover the reasons for the way in which the Universe operates. Hundreds of years of study have led "Science" to produce some very complex theories. These cannot themselves be taught to children and, in any event, Science should involve having an open mind, not an unquestioning acceptance of established theories.

Science is therefore best approached by a simple study and examination of the immediate surroundings. Gradually, explanations can be suggested of observations made.

GARDENING

Gardening is therefore the best possible introduction to Science. Your child learns about the life cycles of plants and animals, the weather, the seasons of the year and about how man can affect the working of Nature.

BOTANY

You can develop the experience gained through gardening by drawing the plants that you grow and looking at the parts of the flower; different types of roots; working out why weeds are so successful etc.

ZOOLOGY

In the same way, you can study the insects in your garden, your household pets and other animals with which you come into contact.

THE ENVIRONMENT

It has been due to the discoveries of Science that man has become a threat to his own environment.

Everyone now accepts that the Environment
is severely threatened by man's activities, and
the Environment is now an issue of prime importance
for your child's generation and for generations
that come after them.

Any study of Science must, therefore, be linked
with the impact that different forms of Scientific
activity have on the Environment. However, it is a
mistake to stress the negative side of man's activities to children, as it can make them depressed,
and give them a sense of hopelessness. Care should
be taken not to introduce Science and Environment
studies to very young children.

ELECTRICITY

One of the most significant scientific discoveries is Electricity. It affects absolutely
every aspect of modern life.

The only way in which Electricity can be under-
stood scientifically is through complex mathematical
formulae, but it is a phenomenon of such significance
that it is worth studying through the effect that
it has on life.

Your child can draw up a list of every way
in which they use electricity; you can study the
principles upon which some of your household app-
liances work; you can study the wiring in your home
and show your child how to change a plug, replace
a light bulb and mend a fuse, and you can discuss
the different ways in which electricity is produced,
and the effect that these have on the environment.

Some children are fascinated by electricity
and you can buy them kits to build a radio or other
simple equipment. They can study for qualifications
to become an amateur radio operator or can experiment
with other forms of electronics.

ASTRONOMY

This is another branch of Science that
interests many children. looking at stars through
a telescope teaches a child a great deal, not only
about Space but also about Optics.

148

PHYSICS

Some areas of Physics are often encountered during other activities. For instance, your child will be aware of different sound frequencies if they are learning a musical instrument. This will be sufficient for some children, while others will want a greater understanding of man's knowledge of Light, Sound, Colour, Mechanics etc. This knowledge is best gained by studying the appropriate books.

CHEMISTRY

If your child is interested in Chemistry, then you can buy them a Chemistry set consisting of chemicals, test-tubes, a spirit burner and beakers.

This is enough to make various different crystals, to study acidity and alkalinity and to experiment with burning different things.

Your child will be as well-equipped as some of the pioneers of chemical discovery a few hundred years ago; will have the advantage of being able to use their equipment whenever they want to; will not be limited for time and will be able to experiment themselves. Assuming that this informal regime allows them to maintain their interest, they can then go on to study modern chemical theories from text-books.

SCIENCE GCSEs

Physics and Chemistry are not taught as much as they used to be as separate subjects. Many young people now do General Science instead, which contains an element of both.

Even though Science is meant to involve an element of questioning and discovery, in practice, GCSEs can do little more than ensure that young people have grasped the basic principles of accepted theories.

A laboratory is therefore not essential to study for Physics, Chemistry and General Science GCSEs, and all these subjects can be covered in one year's study by anyone who already has a lively interest in Science.

The Biological Sciences readily lend themselves to home study and should offer no problems to anyone learning at home.

COMPUTERS

COMPUTERS AND TODAY'S CHILD

Children are, these days, exposed to computers in a way that would have been impossible to imagine even a few years ago.

The majority of parents and teachers assume that the greater contact children have with computers the better, because computers represent the leading edge of modern technology.

Whilst it is true that computers have revolutionised modern work practices and now affect many aspects of modern life, it does not necessarily follow that computers can offer a positive input to the development of a growing child.

Problems can arise in various ways.

HEALTH

Many people, especially children, suffer headaches and other health problems if they sit for too long at a V.D.U. screen.

MENTAL STIMULATION

Like television, computers do not provide a balanced source of stimulation. They do respond to input from the child but without any of the warmth and originality that a child gains from other human beings. This leads children who spend many hours on their computers to develop disturbed psychological and emotional behaviour.

COMPUTER GAMES

Computer games are mentally addictive, tend towards violence and suppress interest in more worthwhile sources of stimulation.

COMPUTER PROGRAMMES

The compact nature of computer discs, the wide availability of computers to children and the weird state of mind that computers engender have led to pornographic and violent computer programmes being circulated amongst children.

WHEN IS THE BEST TIME TO INTRODUCE COMPUTERS?
Given all the disadvantages associated with computers, it is sensible to consider seriously when is the best time for a child to begin using one.

COMPUTERS AND MATHS
Computers are not an aid to learning Arithmetic. It is very hard for a child to learn Arithmetic when they have a machine that can work out the answers for them.

Arithmetic is essential for a later understanding of Mathematics, Computer Programming and any scientific subject, and it is therefore sensible to delay using a computer until a child has a good knowledge of fractions, decimals, percentages etc.

WHEN DOES IT BECOME USEFUL?
For most young people a computer starts to become useful when they can use it to print out essays and project work. It tends to be older children who need to do this sort of work. Younger children like to illustrate their own work and need as much practice in writing as possible, in order to perfect their technique.

WHEN CAN CHILDREN COPE WITH A COMPUTER?
Obviously the older a child is, the more experience they have, and the more interests they will have developed. As a consequence they are less likely to become addicted to computer games and less likely to become mindless slaves to a machine.

PEER GROUP PRESSURE
Home educated children do not suffer from peer group pressure and will not demand a computer because everyone else has one.

WHAT DO THEY NEED TO KNOW?

HOW TO USE IT

Computers are now very easy to use. They come with detailed instruction manuals which you and your child will have no difficulty in following.

There is also an almost unlimited amount of material available in the form of books, magazines and discs that allows you to take your studies further if you become interested.

HOW DOES IT WORK - ELECTRONICS AND COMPUTER PROGRAMMING.

Most people who do use computers have no idea how they work, and young children do not have the background knowledge to be able to understand how a computer works.

If your child has become interested in computers then they may wish to study the principles upon which computers are based. They can study the principles of electronics and it is possible to buy kits with which to build a simple computer.

Computer programming can be learnt quite well from books, as much time is inevitably spent in trial and error and learning from mistakes made - a process which does not lend itself to classroom work.

HISTORY

History is one of the most interesting and rewarding subjects to teach at home. The most logical approach is to start with Ancient History when your child is about nine, and work up to the present day, at a pace that is agreeable to you both. For example:

Age 9/10	Mesopotamians/Egyptians
Age 10/11	Greeks/Alexander the Great
Age 11/12	Romans
Age 12/13	Middle Ages
Age 13/14	Renaissance/Reformation/Voyages of Discovery
Age 14/15	English Civil War. Industrial Revolution
Age 15/16	Twentieth Century

In addition to European History you can consider history through the eyes of other cultures, for example North American Indians, The Chinese, Arab History etc.

There are many different perspectives that you follow as you look at various historical periods for example;

Lives of Ordinary People; Political History (Monarchies, Republics, Democracies); Economic History (Farming, Industry, Cities etc.); Religious History (Christianity, Islam, Buddhism, Hindu); History of War, Empires, Colonialism; Scientific History (Effect of Railways, Cars, Planes, Telephones Television, Nuclear Power etc.) and Social History (The Growth of Cities, Welfare Systems, Work Patterns Role of Men and Women in Society).

You cannot hope to make notes and write essays on all these subjects, but by talking about these things you help your child to understand the world as it is today, and to be able to interpret all the information that comes through news media about the events taking place around the world.

GEOGRAPHY

The best way to approach Geography is to start with local surroundings that are familiar to your child and gradually expand outwards, eventually to encompass the whole world.

The sort of things that you can consider, in relation to each area studied, are:

Landscape   – Hills, mountains, rivers, Proximity to the sea etc.

Weather   – Prevailing winds. Level of rainfall, Hours of sun etc.

Geology   – Soil types. Underlying rock formations. The effect of the Ice Ages.

People   – What sort of people life there? How many? Population levels. Ethnic and cultural characteristics.

Economy   – Traditional farming and industry. Modern sources of wealth.

An overall scheme that you can follow could be:

Age 9/10	Local Geography
Age 10/11	United Kingdom
Age 11/12	Europe. European Community. Eastern Europe.
Age 12/13	North America/Australasia
Age 13/14	Asia. China. Japan. India. Pakistan.
Age 14/15	Africa. South America.
Age 15/16	Overall World Geography

In the later years of this scheme there will be a considerable overlap between History and Geography, and you may wish to link them together, maybe concentrating on European History but also giving a clear picture of the current interdependence of all the peoples of the world.

RELIGION

This subject has not been specifically discussed in this book, but the moral and religious views of a parent will obviously influence all the work that they do with their child.

Schools often encounter real problems in communicating moral values because so many of the children who attend feel that they are the victims of an immoral regime.

This problem does not arise when a child is taught at home, and you will find that discussions about the nature of right and wrong, good and evil and the existence of God occur naturally in the course of day to day work.

SUMMARY

Other subjects, such as languages and craftwork, that were discussed earlier in relation to younger children can be continued and developed with older children.

Children that have been taught at home from a young age can be expected to maintain an interest in a wide range of subjects - although not necessarily working at all of them all the time.

Children who have been to school for a time, on the other hand, may have blocks about certain subjects, which may make them unable or unwilling to tackle them.

EDUCATION AFTER SIXTEEN

Education is only compulsory up to the age of 16, but it is becoming increasingly difficult for young people to find work, and most of them therefore go on to some form of Further Education. Home educated children have various options.

WORK + STUDY,- BASED AT HOME.

For many home educated children the ideal may be to continue and develop the work that they have been doing already. Hopefully they will already have projects bringing in some income, or else be involved in some work with their parents. Once they are 16 there need be no restriction placed upon how much time they spend on this work, and they may be able to develop it into a reasonable source of income.

In addition to this they may well want to continue their education. This may be simply for pleasure or else to gain knowledge or qualifications that they feel will be useful in their work.

All the resources previously discussed such as books, correspondence courses, evening classes etc. are available to aid this form of study. In addition, young people can go to college for one or two days per week to get qualifications in a range of skills and subjects.

A-LEVELS

Young people that have a particular interest in a subject or who wish to go to University may wish to study for A-levels.

These have fairly demanding syllabuses and if more than one is being attempted at a time, they will require more or less full-time study.

STUDY AT HOME

A-levels can be studied for at home and there is no reason why a young person who has successfully mastered the techniques of home study to pass their GCSEs should not do well at A level. They will find it easier if you can continue to support them by developing your own interests in the subjects that they have chosen. You may even wish to sit the 'A' levels yourself!

STUDY AT SCHOOL/COLLEGE

The atmosphere is Sixth Forms, Sixth Form Colleges and Colleges of Further Education, where attendance is not compulsory, is often a lot better than that in schools.

If your child does wish to pass A levels and go on to University, or another course in Higher Education, then they may wish to enter one of these local educational establishments.

UNIVERSITY

Historically, a University degree is the most valuable asset in the job market and University graduates, on average, earn significantly more than the rest of the population.

In addition, University may offer a young person a unique opportunity to study and develop their interest in a chosen subject.

Young people wishing to go to University have to achieve as good A level results as they can, as these provide virtually the sole criteria for University entrance.

Young people educated at home will find themselves increasingly at an advantage over school educated children as they go through the educational system. They do not have to unlearn the structured learning system required at school, and will already know how to organise themselves and to take responsibility for their own studies.

FINDING WORK

The primary aim of our educational system is said to be to prepare young people for work.

Home education is bound to encourage initiative and a level of self reliance that is absent in a child who has had to learn to adapt their expectations to the limitations imposed by working, as one of a class, to a predetermined curriculum.

Whatever level of qualifications your child has progressed to, the overall experience of Home Education will make them an interesting proposition to a potential employer.

Home educated children are usually successful in achieving their goals and in finding the kind of work in which they are interested.

SECTION IV

USEFUL INFORMATION

USEFUL BOOKS

There are obviously thousands of books available, many of which are of use to Home Educators. You will have to look for ones that are of interest to you and your child.

The following list gives a few books which have been found to be particularly useful and which may give you some inspiration if you find yourself getting stuck. They are relatively easy to come across and their popularity should ensure that they remain in print.

GENERAL INTEREST
School is Not Compulsory (Education Otherwise)
The National Curriculum, Charles Hymas (Sunday Times)
Festivals Family and Food, Diana Carey and Judy Large
(Hawthorn Press)
Assessment Papers in English, Reasoning and Maths
J M Bond (Nelson)

CRAFT
The Doll Book, Karin Neuschütz (Floris)
Making Dolls, S Reinckens (Floris)
Dryad Leaflets — available from Craft shops.
The Children's Year, S Cooper (Hawthorn Press)

MUSIC
Sing, Clap and Play the Recorder, Heather Cox and
Garth Rickard (Macmillan Education)
John W Schaum Piano Course,
(International Music Publications)

SCIENCE
The Young Scientist Investigates,
(Oxford University Press)
Eyewitness Books (Dorling Kindersley)

ARITHMETIC
Rules of Maths, Connor and Soper (Oriflamme)

HISTORY
The Usborne Illustrated World History Series(Usborne)
The Story of Britain, R J Unstead (A&C Black)

GEOGRAPHY
Collins-Longman Atlas for Secondary Schools
(Collins-Longman)
Britain Maps and Mapwork, John Moser (Nelson)

ENGLISH
Learn Good English, W D Wright (Nisbet)
The Faber Book of Children's Verse (Faber and Faber)

RELIGION
The All-Colour Children's Bible (Hamlyn)
Prince Siddhartha, Jonathan Landaw and Janet Brooke
(Wisdom - distributed by Element Books)
Puffin Classics, Roger Lancelyn Green (a series which
retells stories from classic mythology)

LANGUAGES
Usborne Language Guides (Usborne)
Recueil de Poemes, Chants, Jeux et Comptines
-Available from Botton Bookshop (see
address list). Some knowledge of Fre-
nch is needed to understand it.
Hugo Language Courses - very useful for parents and
teenagers learning a new language.

GCSE REVISION GUIDES
Letts GCSE Revision Guides (Letts)
Keyfacts GCSE Passbooks (Letts)
Longman Revise Guides (Longman)
Macmillan Master Series (Macmillan)

USEFUL ADDRESSES

GENERAL

EDUCATION OTHERWISE   PO BOX 120 Leamington Spa
                                 Warwickshire CU32 7ER

BBC EDUCATION INFORMATION   White City
                                        London W12 77S

CHANNEL 4 EDUCATION TELEVISION   PO Box 100
                                            Warwick CU34 6TZ

YOUNG ORNITHOLOGISTS CLUB   The Lodge Sandy
(Junior R.S.P.B.)   Bedfordshire SG19 2DL

JUNIOR ROYAL SOC. FOR NATURE   The Green Waterside Sth
CONSERVATION (WATCH)   Lincoln LN5 7JR

NATIONAL LISTENING LIBRARY   12 Slant Street
                                      London SE1 1QH
(Provides tapes for anyone who has difficulty reading)

DEPARTMENT FOR EDUCATION   Mowden Hall Staindrop Road
                                   Darlington Co Durham DL3 9BG

BOTTON BOOKSHOP   Botton Village Danby
                        Whitby North Yorkshire YO21 2NJ
(Specialises in Steiner books and has many imported
titles not easily available elsewhere. It has a
good mail order service.)

PUBLISHERS

The following publishers offer a range of educational books and most of them would be happy to provide you with a catalogue. You can order direct if you do not have a good local bookshop.

USBORNE PUBLISHING LTD   Usborne House 83 Saffron Hill
London EC1N 8RT

HAWTHORN PRESS   Bankfield House 13 WallBridge
Stroud GL5 3JA

FLORIS BOOKS   21 Napier Road
Edinburgh

MACMILLAN EDUCATION LTD   Houndmills Basingstoke
Hampshire RG21 2XS

THOMAS NELSON and SONS LTD   51 York Place
Edinburgh EH1 3JD

DORLING KINDERSLEY   9 Henrietta Steet
Covent Garden London WC2E 8PS

OXFORD UNIVERSITY PRESS   Walton Street
Oxford OX2 6DP

LETTS EDUCATIONAL LTD   Aldine Hse 142-144 Uxbridge Rd
London W12 8AW

LONGMAN GROUP UK LTD   Longman House Burnt Mill
Harlow Essex CM20 2JE

JAMES NISBET & CO LTD   Digswell Place
Welwyn Garden City Herts

ORIFLAMME PUBLISHING LTD   60 Charteris Road
London N4 3AB

EXAMINATION BOARDS

The country has been divided up between various GCSE boards. However, you are not obliged to use your local board and are quite at liberty to enter examinations set by other boards if you consider them to be better suited to your requirements.

NEA (Northern England)   12 Harter Street
                           Manchester M1 6HL

MEG (Midlands)   Robins Wood Hse
                           Aspley Nottingham NG8 3NR

LEAG (London & East Anglia) Stewart House
                           32 Russell Square
                           London WC1B 5DN

SEG (Southern England)   Stag Hill House
                           Guildford Surrey GU2 5XJ

WJEC (Wales)   245 Western Avenue
                           Cardiff CFF 2YZ

NISEAC (Northern Ireland) Beechill Hse Beechill Rd
                           Belfast BT8 4RS

SCOTTISH EXAMINATIONS BOARD Ironmills Rd Dalkeith
                           Midlothian EH22 1BR

NOTE

Britain is one of very few countries which set external examinations for sixteen year olds. It is a system that has not worked well for some time and every attempt to improve it seems to make things worse. Consequently the system is altered more and more frequently.

Changes in progress at the time of going to press include changing the grading system from letters (A to G) to numbers (1 to 10) and trying to tighten up the assessment of coursework. This may affect external candidates and you should contact the examination board for up to date information.

VOCATIONAL QUALIFICATIONS

BUISNESS & TECHNOLOGY EDUCATION COUNCIL (BTEC)
Central Hse Upper Woburn Place
London WC1H 0HH

CITY & GUILDS of LONDON INSTITUTE
76 Portland Place
London W1N 4AA

RSA EXAMINATIONS BOARD   Progress House
Westwood Way
Coventry CV4 8HS3

NATIONAL COUNCIL FOR VOCATIONAL QUALIFICATIONS (NCVQ)
222 Euston Road
London NW1 2BZ

CORRESPONDENCE COURSES

COUNCIL FOR THE ACCREDITATION OF CORRESPONDENCE
COLLEGES   27 Marylebone Road
London NW1 5JS

ASSOCIATION OF BRITISH CORRESPONDENCE COLLEGES
6 Francis Grove
London SW19 4DT

WORLDWIDE EDUCATION SERVICE   35 Belgrage Square
London SW1X 8QB

THE OPEN UNIVERSITY   Walton Hall
Milton Keynes MK7 6AA

SUPPLIERS OF EDUCATIONAL MATERIALS

Local shops are probably the best source of educational materials and they will often give a discount if you explain that you teach your children at home.You may find the following suppliers helpful, however, if you cannot find what you need locally.

NES ARNOLD LTD Ludlow Hill Road West Bridgford
NOTTINGHAM NG2 6HD

SHEFFIELD PURCHASING ORGANISATION Staniforth Road
SHEFFIELD S9 3GZ

THOMAS NELSON and SONS LTD Nelson House Mayfield Road
WALTON-ON-THAMES Surrey KT12 4BR

THE ORGANIC GARDENING CATALOGUE Coombelands House
ADDLESTONE Surrey KT15 1HY

LEARNING DEVELOPMENT AIDS Duke Street WISBECH Cambs.
PE13 2AE
(especially for children with learning difficulties)

PLAYAWAYS SUPPLIES(Scotland)LTD Annick Industrial Est.
Shettleston GLASGOW G32 0HS

INDEX

Primrose Lane Educational Press is an independent publishing company dedicated to producing books and pamphlets of use to home educating parents.

If you want to be kept informed about future publications, please use the order form below.

- -

Please send me information about future publications

Name: _____

Address: _____

_____

_____

Send to: Primrose Lane Educational Press P.O. Box 154
         Pocklington York YO4 1YW

- -